THE BOOK OF ESTHER

Also by Leanna Brodie

For Home and Country
Schoolhouse
The Vic

All available from Talonbooks

THE **BOOK** OF **ESTHER**

Leanna Brodie

Talonbooks

Talonbooks
P.O. Box 2076, Vancouver, British Columbia, Canada V6B 3S3
www.talonbooks.com

Typeset in Minion and printed and bound in Canada.
Printed on 100% post-consumer recycled paper.
First printing: 2012
Typeset by Typesmith. Cover design by Brian Houle.

The publisher gratefully acknowledges the financial support of the Canada Council
for the Arts; the Government of Canada through the Canada Book Fund; and the
Province of British Columbia through the British Columbia Arts Council and the
Book Publishing Tax Credit for our publishing activities.

LIBRARY AND ARCHIVES CANADA CATALOGUING IN PUBLICATION

Brodie, Leanna, 1966–
      The book of Esther / Leanna Brodie.

A play.
ISBN 978-0-88922-682-1

      I. Title.

PS8553.R6337B66 2012   C812'.6   C2011-908724-3

For my dearest friend, Elizabeth d'Anjou, not in spite of but because of the fact that we disagree about everything.

For her huge-hearted family, who took me in, as they did so many others.

For my loyal and loving stepfather, Jack Lynch, who passed away during the final rehearsals for this play. Jack, I hope you would have liked it.

At last all the children ran away from home and were brought up by an old spinster who lived down the street.

— JAMES REANEY
Twelve Letters to a Small Town

The Book of Esther, by Leanna Brodie, premiered on August 6, 2010, at the Blyth Festival, under the artistic direction of Eric Coates.

Cast (in order of speaking):

ANTHEA DALZELL: Marion Day
TODD WISHART: Brad Rudy
A.D.: Nathan Carroll
ESTHER DALZELL: Maggie Blake
SETH DALZELL: Eric Coates

Director: Leah Cherniak
Costume and Set Designer: Victoria Wallace
Lighting Designer: Rebecca Picherack
Sound Designer: Marc Desormeaux
Video Designer: Cameron Davis
Stage Manager: Dini Conte
Assistant Stage Manager: Amy Jewell

A second production premiered at the Festival Players of Prince Edward County, under the artistic direction of Sarah Phillips, on July 13, 2011.

Cast (in order of speaking):

ANTHEA DALZELL: Leanna Brodie
TODD WISHART: Gordon Miller
A.D.: Mark Rotil
ESTHER DALZELL: Abigail Fernandes
SETH DALZELL: Roger Shank

Director: Brad Rudy
Costume Designer: Jennifer Triemstra-Johnston
Lighting Designer: Raha Javanfar
Set Designer: Glenn Davidson
Stage Manager: Krista Hansen-Robitschek
House Technician: Rob Robitaille

Characters

TODD WISHART, mid-forties
ESTHER DALZELL, fifteen
ANTHEA DALZELL, early forties
A.D., seventeen
SETH DALZELL, mid-forties

Introduction

Leanna Brodie told me once that she wanted to write a play about rural Ontario's number-one export: youth. I liked the idea the same way an artsy kid from, say, the rural community of Wingham likes the idea of moving to the city of Toronto. I gave Leanna the green light and urged her to let me know as soon as she had something that was ready to read. We had just worked together on the extremely successful premiere of her play *Schoolhouse*, which the Blyth Festival had commissioned and developed during the previous two years. Knowing that Leanna had a strong and intuitive understanding of our audience, I went back to my daily chores, confident that she would deliver something germane to our audience and mandate, both.

Time passed ... Leanna called to tell me that the characters in her play, as they so often do, had ideas of their own. It turned out that the play was not only about the exodus of rural youth, but also about the chasm between evangelical Christians and just about everyone else. In short, it was about them and us.

The Blyth Festival thrives in a rural village with a population that hovers close to a thousand. On a good day, when both the matinee and the evening show have sold out, the number of people who go through the theatre nearly equals the population of the village itself. Our host village – Blyth, Ontario – boasts a grocery store, a branch of the Royal Canadian Legion, a diner, a hotel, and a small but eclectic combination of family businesses that fill the two blocks of retail space. And there are churches: Anglican, United, Christian Reform, Church of God, and Living Water Christian Fellowship. The Catholic church closed a few years ago, but the others continue to thrive – particularly the Christian Reform church that boasts a growing congregation and youth participation that rivals the local hockey league. Coming from a singularly agnostic background, I'm always confounded how our village could barely support one watering hole while five churches thrived. But the Christian community is an essential part of the Blyth Festival's core audience and we have always been very careful where we tread when it comes to issues of faith.

As Leanna developed her new script, it was clear that the characters would continue to drive their individual agendas. Furthermore, I could see that this simple narrative of a teen runaway was quickly growing into an epic history of family and community. Set in the 1980s against the backdrop of the emerging gay culture, *The Book of Esther* was poised to resonate strongly with the generation who had struggled with the idea of inclusion versus mere tolerance or, worse, outright ostracism. Leanna's singular gift is her ability to radiate respect and compassion. Because of this gift, she was able to gain the mutual respect and trust of people representing all sides of the issue. The result was a beautifully balanced story of love, loss, and respect for divergent beliefs.

I will always treasure my experience with this play. I learned from it in every aspect: as an artistic director, as a dramaturge, and as an actor. But the most important lesson came a few months after the season had closed. A volunteer who works regularly as an usher came into the office one day, needing to talk. A stalwart member of the Christian Reform church, she told us that her best friend had recently come out and was now living openly as a lesbian. Given the rigidity of the volunteer's faith, this was extremely difficult for her to embrace, but she went on to explain that she would not turn her back on her friend. "A few years ago," she said, "I could not have remained friends with her. But now … because of that play … I am able to see it differently."

We produce new work here each year. Like *The Book of Esther,* some plays get terrific reviews, some get standing ovations, and some are nominated for prestigious awards. And I wouldn't be surprised if this play joins the awards list. Yet none of these accolades surpasses Leanna's achievement of changing the way that one person saw the world.

ERIC COATES
Artistic Director, Blyth Festival
November 2011

A Note on Layout

The conventions used in this text, from simultaneous dialogue in two columns to beats and pauses, will be familiar to people who read modern plays – except for one. This script convention may be more familiar to readers of comic books, which were very popular in 1981, the time setting for *The Book of Esther*. Throughout this play, as in many plays, DIALOGUE IN CAPITAL LETTERS indicates words directed outward – extroverted words, delivered to or *at* other people with heightened volume or intensity. Conversely, DIALOGUE IN SMALL CAPS is used here for words murmured to a confidant or spoken almost unconsciously to oneself. Like all introverts, they can be just as intense as the extroverts.

Setting

ACT I

The main set consists of a slightly crumbling rental apartment in a marginal downtown neighbourhood, summer 1981. On one part of the stage, we are in a kitchen with a large open window. Any number of kitchen things may be on display. Wherever there are realistic kitchen details, there should be an overlay of fabulousness: naked Ken dolls, paper fans, and other thrift-shop exotica. Pride of place, however, is given to a mosaic on the kitchen wall, incorporating a collection of the famous series of Wade miniature ceramics known to generations of Canadians as "Red Rose figurines." Adjoining the kitchen is a hallway that leads to the rest of the apartment, including the front door. The other entrance to the kitchen leads onto a rooftop deck complete with plants and ramshackle chairs. A stairway leads up to the deck from the back alley.

ACT II

The main set consists of a slightly crumbling brick-and-gingerbread farmhouse near the village of Baker's Creek, summer 1981. We see exactly the same kitchen as in Act I, except that all campy, ironic, urban elements have been replaced by family photos, children's drawings, and Christian religious items. In place of the mosaic is a wall-mounted cabinet whose sole purpose is to display an intact collection of Red Rose figurines. Adjoining the kitchen is a hallway that leads to the rest of the house, including a set of stairs leading to the second floor as well as the front door. The other entrance to the kitchen leads onto a covered porch complete with plants and old chairs. Steps lead up to the porch from the yard.

All other locations can be created with lighting and one or two simple pieces, as needed.

Nowhere is there any obligation to naturalism, or to anything beyond what is required by the story. (For example, no one ever seems to use the kitchen sink.)

Act I **Scene 1**

As the lights dim and come up again we hear a couple of verses of "O Lamb of God," in the sprightly rendition of a child:

Just as I am, without one plea,
But that Thy blood was shed for me,
And that Thou bid'st me come to Thee,
O Lamb of God, I come, I come!

Just as I am, though tossed about
With many a conflict, many a doubt,
Fightings and fears within, without,
O Lamb of God, I come, I come!

Lights up on ANTHEA teaching her Sunday school class.

ANTHEA
Kids, what do most people want?

Beat.

We want to know how to live a good life. We want to understand who we are and where we came from, why things are the way they are, and where do we go from here. And God understands that. God knows it's a long road ahead of us, so He sent His only Son with a map.

She holds up a Bible.

Yet most of us refuse to use it! Isn't that crazy? Does that make any sense?

Beat.

There are all kinds of reasons why people get lost. But you know what I don't understand? What I don't understand are the people who have the map, they've read the map, but then they pull a U-turn on the highway to heaven and go pell-mell in the other direction! Now I ask you, for all the thrill of flying full tilt down a wrong-way road, for all the shiny, sparkly trash you might find there … how can any of it possibly compare with going home to Jesus? That's why those who have never been born again are not the greatest disappointment to the Lord. The greatest disappointment to the Lord is when we who have been born again, who've been washed in the Blood, we, in full knowledge of His plan for us … pull a U-ey on the road to heaven, and floor it back the other way. Then we not only disappoint Jesus, but betray Him. Then we see our Lord suffering and bleeding on the cross – pick up a hammer – and drive in another nail.

Act I **Scene 2**

Early Monday evening, late June 1981. The kitchen of
TODD's apartment. Voices are heard offstage.

TODD

… and the TV is in here. This is called a futon, you open the frame …

His voice becomes strained.

… like this, please make it up every day, if you're here next month we'll
trade rooms for the Royal Wedding, I must watch Charles and Di make
the biggest mistake of their lives. Please don't smoke inside, I don't
care what you're smoking or why, but the cats hate the smell and they
protest by shitting under my bed, which is just unpleasant for everybody.
Speaking of unpleasant for everybody, here's the bathroom. Please don't
flush your rags, and please do wash your pits every day whether you
think you need to or not. Please brush your teeth, on the same principle.

As TODD speaks, he and ESTHER enter the room. TODD
is an attractive middle-aged man in cut-off shorts; ESTHER
is a long-haired, rather grim-looking teenager wearing a
unisex plaid shirt, jeans, a John Deere cap placed somewhat
askew, and steel-toed boots.

It's only the two of us at the moment, but there'll be another of you sooner
or later. There's always another one … do your dishes when you use them:
do I look like your mama, I do not look like your mama, even if I did look
like your mama, you should treat your mama better.

Beat.

Here's the fridge. If it's marked "no," don't eat it. If it's not marked "no,"
don't waste my time asking if you can eat it, eat it. If you buy something
and you don't want anyone to eat it, mark it "no." Everyone who's ever
stayed here knows what that means. Yes, some of them come back.

Beat.

Marker. Yours will be the … blue one. Write on the masking tape if it's the good Tupperware. If it's a margarine tub, the marker is fine.

Beat. TODD sees ESTHER staring at the Red Rose mosaic.

The mosaic? Uh-huh. I used to have this little display case full of Red Rose figurines. Tacky as spit, of course, but I couldn't get rid of them; they're about the only thing my mother left me except for a lifelong hatred of bingo. The best part is, she didn't even drink tea. She'd buy the box, fish out the little statue, and chuck the tea into the cupboard. I guess it was the only pretty thing in her day. The one thing she could look forward to. Well, that and the whisky. When I went to clean out her apartment, she had thirty full boxes of Red Rose tea, and fifty empty bottles of Black Velvet whisky. Good old Mom.

Beat.

Anyway, there was this one boy with – how shall I put this – a little anger problem, and I wouldn't let him have drugs in my place, so he threw the whole case on the floor and stomped on it. Then I said to him: "What are you planning to do with the pieces, Cupcake? Because the only excuse for destroying something pretty is to turn it into something gorgeous." So he made this. That's when I knew that he –

> *A teenaged boy – slight of build, with spiked hair and a torn T-shirt – vaults in through the kitchen window. TODD yells in surprise, while ESTHER screams and runs out of the room. A.D. brushes himself off and checks for damage.*

A.D.
(*to TODD*) Hey.

TODD
Speak of the devil. Perfect timing, as always. (*calling*) Esther, it's all right. This is A.D. He lives here. Sometimes. Unfortunately. (*to A.D.*) You and your dramatic entrances. Where's your key?

A.D.
Lost it. I think. Half of Queen Street has your key. Don't know why you even bother with a lock.

TODD
Perhaps the other half of Queen Street doesn't meet the stringent standards of the establishment. (*calling*) Esther, it's okay. Really. A.D.'s a big pussy … cat. Come back and I'll introduce you to the little dickens.

TODD moves to close the window.

A.D.

(*quickly*) You might not want to go near the window right now.

TODD

Oh, no. Really? What is it now? Cops? Boyfriends? Tricks?

A.D. surreptitiously peers through the window.

A.D.

And ... we're done. (*as ESTHER comes back in*) Who's this one?

TODD

Esther. She's from back home. Esther ... uh ... (*to ESTHER*) Have you not told me your last name, honey, or am I losing my mind?

ESTHER shakes her head. Beat.

Okay ... A.D., this is Esther. Esther, A.D.

Beat. ESTHER seems a little overwhelmed.

A.D.

Earth to Helen Keller. Are you getting all this?

A.D. points to himself.

AYYYY ... DEE. So why'd you run away from the farm? Did your cousin start looking at you funny?

Beat. ESTHER is still struggling to answer.

TODD

Now, now, lots of time to torture the new girl. You staying?

A.D. nods.

I'll clear out the closet for you. Don't, I've heard it six hundred times and it wasn't even funny the once.

A.D.

Hey, Todd, she's still trying to talk. Is she too inbred to talk or something?

TODD

Button it, A.D.

A.D.

(slowly) WHY'D YOU RUN AWAY? ARE YOU PREGNANT OR
SOMETHING?

Beat.

DID SOMEONE GET YOU KNOCKED UP?

ESTHER

Why? You offering?

TODD and A.D. laugh.

A.D.

I like this one. Dad, can we keep her, can we keep her?

TODD

I am not your father.

A.D.

Fine ... Mom.

TODD

I am definitely not your mother.

A.D. imitates TODD, as by rote.

A.D.

"Do I look like your mama, I do not look like your mama, even if I did
look like your mama ..."

A.D. laughs; ESTHER smiles a little.

TODD

Very, very funny, A.D. You got so much hot air, go inflate the mattress.

A.D.

(leaving) Did you ever find the foot pump after – what was the last one
again? "Simon" or something?

TODD

(calling after him) No. Try under the futon. If it's not there, you'll have to
do it the hard way. You know ... (as Bacall) Put your lips together – and
blow. (to ESTHER) Do you want to talk, honey?

ESTHER shakes her head.

ESTHER

They think I'm on a trip.

> *Beat.*

My parents. They think I'm on the school trip. Till Thursday night. So. There's no problem with ... anything. For now.

> *Beat.*

I couldn't do it. I was standing in the parking lot, beside the bus, everyone was getting in, and I just ... I couldn't go home, and I couldn't get on the bus.

TODD

(*noncommittally*) Uh-huh.

> *Beat.*

ESTHER

I'm going to ... I'm going to go watch TV for a bit.

> *TODD watches ESTHER go into the other room. A.D. comes back in.*

A.D.

You're out of pillowcases again ...

> *Beat.*

Todd? What's wrong?

TODD

Oh ... it's nothing, just ... nothing. She reminds me of someone I used to know.

Act I **Scene 3**

The next day, Tuesday. Inside a subway station, train level. A.D. and ESTHER come on. ESTHER is holding samosas in a little white takeout sleeve. A.D. is holding a takeout bag.

A.D.

… so this is the platform. Once you get on the train, if there are no seats, hold on to something because it will jerk to a stop and you'll fall down.

A.D. shows ESTHER a subway transfer.

Hold on to this because you might need to transfer to a bus.

Beat.

You getting all this? Because you're on your own from now on. I do basic training for all Todd's strays, but I'm not taking them for walks. No offence.

Beat.

You okay?

ESTHER

Yeah. Just … really hungry. And these … things … smell so good.

A.D.

Samosas. Go on, dig in. You can eat in the subway, everyone does.

A.D. is about to inhale his samosas, but notices ESTHER quietly saying a little prayer before eating hers. Bemused, A.D. stops and watches.

ESTHER

AMEN.

ESTHER bites lustily into her samosa.

A.D.

You're not from some Looney Tunes cult thing, are you? Because that stuff freaks me right out –

ESTHER

– It's not a – ah – ahh – aaah …

> *ESTHER's eyes bulge and she starts fanning her face with her hands, as if that will neutralize the unfamiliar blaze inside her mouth.*

A.D.

Bit of a kick, eh?

ESTHER

(*gasping*) Water …

A.D.

Water only swishes the heat around. You need rice.

> *He finds a container in his takeout bag and hands it to ESTHER. She almost tears it open, stuffing rice into her mouth with her hands.*

I must have given you my samosas; I ordered yours White People Mild. Here.

> *He hands her his packet of samosas. ESTHER bites a chunk out of one.*

ESTHER

It's not some Looney Tunes cult.

A.D.

What?

ESTHER

My church. It's not a – ahh – aaoooaaah …

> *This time she practically screams and rolls around on the ground in pain.*

A.D.

I guess that *was* yours. You really can't handle your spices, huh … have you ever seen a pepper?

> *ESTHER gasps, cramming rice into her mouth by the handful and swallowing, until the burning begins to subside.*

ESTHER
My church is not a cult. I JUST NEED TO FIGURE OUT ... WHAT'S THE BABY JESUS ... AND WHAT'S THE BATHWATER.

A.D.
Come again?

> *The rice is finally putting out the fire; ESTHER sighs with relief.*

ESTHER
HAH.

A.D.
Look, I'll eat them both and we'll go find you a burger.

ESTHER
No.

> *Beat.*

It's good. But next time, more rice.

> *She tucks into his samosas, wiping her tears with her sleeve. A.D. looks at her admiringly.*

A.D.
Wow, Mary. You're gonna make it after all.

Act I **Scene 4**

Friday morning, several days later. Doorbell.

TODD
    (*off*) CAN SOMEONE GET THAT?

        No response.

Of course not. Because that would be too much to ask.

        The doorbell rings repeatedly. TODD, in a dressing gown,
        drying his hair with a towel, can be seen crossing the
        hallway and going toward the door, muttering. After a
        moment the door bangs open and ANTHEA bursts into the
        kitchen. TODD stops in the doorway, poleaxed. ANTHEA –
        suddenly seeing him there in his dressing gown – is almost
        equally nonplussed.

TODD
    Anthea.

        Beat.

So you're … and she's …

        Beat.

    Huh.

ANTHEA
    (*snapping out of it*) She's here, isn't she.

        ESTHER peeks into the kitchen, sees ANTHEA, and flees.

ESTHER! Esther, come out here, please.

        Offstage, a door slams.

Esther, you can stay in that room as long as you like, I'll be here when you
get out.

TODD
　Actually –

ANTHEA
　– You are fifteen years old and you are my responsibility, so you can come
　out here and discuss this like a big girl, or I can call the police and you
　can come home with them.

TODD
　Now just a cotton-pickin' –

ANTHEA
　– I'm going to pick up the phone on the count of three. ONE –

TODD
　– This is my home, and –

ANTHEA
　– You think I won't do it? TWO –

TODD
　– You know, I have slept with a lot of lawyers –

ANTHEA
　– My family. My business. You stay out of it, or –

　　　ESTHER appears.

Oh, Esther. Praise Him, praise Jesus.

　　　She takes ESTHER's hands and immediately closes her eyes.

Heavenly Father, we humbly thank Thee for returning our daughter to us
safe and sound. Amen.

　　　ANTHEA opens her eyes and looks at ESTHER.

I'm glad you're all right, Esther. Now get in the truck.

TODD
　Excuse me –

ANTHEA
　– This is none of your –

TODD
　– It is now. Obviously.

ANTHEA
>Let's go.

>*She tries to steer ESTHER toward the door, but ESTHER*
>*refuses.*

(*to ESTHER*) Do you know what it was like, standing there yesterday in
the parking lot with the other parents, waiting for you to get off the bus?
And waiting. And waiting. Like an idiot. Till the last kid got off. Panicking.
Crying. I called the police: "Start a search party, she's been abducted." We
found your message on our machine: "Don't worry. I'm okay. I'm not
telling you where I am." The minute we got the story out of Simon Coyte,
how he came here when he ... we jumped in the truck to bring you home.
And if that barn alarm goes off and no one's there to hear it, we could lose
five thousand birds – is that what you want? You want us to be finished?

>*SETH, a powerfully built man in farm overalls and rubber*
>*boots, bursts into the room. He sees TODD, and they lock*
>*eyes for a moment; but then SETH sees ESTHER.*

SETH
>Essie. You okay?

>*She nods.*

What happened?

>*She hesitates a moment, shakes her head.*

Someone ... do somethin' to you?

>*She shakes her head, more definitely.*

I'm real sorry you're havin' a hard time, Essie. But we need to get back to
the farm. Come home and I promise I'll fix it, whatever it is.

ANTHEA
>She –

>*Without looking away from ESTHER, SETH gestures to*
>*ANTHEA to be silent. ESTHER hesitates, looks toward*
>*TODD – who is staring at SETH, momentarily at a loss for*
>*words – looks at the floor, and nods.*

ESTHER
>OKAY.

SETH

(*to ESTHER*) Good girl. Need to go get your things at all?

She nods.

Let's go.

TODD

Esther! Esther, are you sure this is what you –

SETH

– NO ONE WAS TALKIN' TO YOU, YOU SICK PIECE OF –

SETH, his arm around ESTHER, is walking her toward the hall. A.D., clothed but sleepy, appears at the doorway. On registering the scene before him, he snaps awake and blocks SETH's way.

A.D.

– Whoa.

He pulls a jackknife out of his pocket.

Let go of her.

ANTHEA

SETH –

SETH is about to go for A.D., but ESTHER stops him.

ESTHER

– Dad, NO! He's my friend! (*to A.D.*) He's my dad.

A.D.

So?

SETH

(*to A.D.*) WHO IN BLAZES ARE YOU?

TODD

This is A.D.

A.D.

Short for "Angel of Death."

SETH

WHAT KIND OF A NAME IS THAT?

A.D.

    It's my name, Major Scumbag. Wanna see why?

TODD

    (recovering) All right, EVERYBODY STAND DOWN. The Testosterone
    Derby is over. *(to A.D.)* You. Give me that.

        A.D. closes the jackknife and hands it over.

    No knives in my house, ever. You know that. Big strong man wants to
    protect the little girl? Chivalry lives, huh? Honestly, sometimes you're so
    stupid I could swear you're straight. Now get out.

        A.D. leaves; TODD turns on SETH.

    And you –

ANTHEA

    – Seth, what on earth? Were you trying to get her killed?

SETH

    I was protectin' her –

ANTHEA

    – If you hadn't been yelling again for no reason –

SETH

    – He had a knife –

ANTHEA

    – He's a child, Seth! Why do you always make things worse?

        *ESTHER flees to the deck. Her parents move to follow her,
        but TODD stops them.*

TODD

    Give her a minute. *(calling out to the deck)* ESTHER, YOU HANG
    TIGHT, HONEY, OKAY? I'LL BE OUT IN A LITTLE BIT.

        SETH is about to push past him.

    Don't. I could take you back in Junior "B" and I fight a lot dirtier now.

        Beat.

    All right, would someone care to inform me what on earth is going on?
    Because if you drag her back like this, she will be on my doorstep again in
    two minutes. Or somewhere you'll like even less. And you can take that
    to the bank.

Beat.

(*to SETH*) Repark the Ford and call about the chickens. You're going to be here a while.

SETH
(*to ANTHEA*) I'll be in the truck.

He leaves. Beat.

ANTHEA
What am I going to do?

TODD
I don't know.

Meanwhile, on the deck, ESTHER is staring into space when A.D. pops up over the railing.

A.D.
Hey.

ESTHER shrieks, covers her mouth.

ESTHER
Please don't do that.

A.D.
Oh. So, does your dad hit you?

ESTHER
What? Why? Does yours?

A.D.
That's not an answer.

ESTHER
Neither is that.

A.D.
Did he hit you? Cuz if he did, I am gonna hurt him.

ESTHER
What? Calm down, okay? You barely even know me.

A.D.
Oh, I know you.

Beat.

ESTHER
    I left. Okay? I just – left.

A.D.
    (*leaving*) Yep. He's a dead man.

ESTHER
    WAIT! Come back here!

        He does.

    Now look me in the eye.

        He does.

    My dad didn't hit me.

        Beat.

A.D.
    Your mother?

ESTHER
    No! Look – let it go, okay? And don't, like, kill my dad. Just … wait here with me.

A.D.
    Wait for what?

ESTHER
    I don't know.

        Beat.

A.D.
    So they didn't hit you.

ESTHER
    No. Jeez.

A.D.
    Hmm. Be simpler if they did.

        ESTHER looks at him inquiringly.

A.D.

> If your dad hit you, it'd be easy for you to stay. Student welfare, get you set up in your own place, the whole bit. Cops get right off your case the minute your old man puts you in a cast ... trust me.

Beat.

> You're not gonna set him up for assault.

ESTHER shakes her head.

> But you don't wanna go home either.

ESTHER emphatically shakes her head.

> Then there's only one choice: come with me, little girl.

ESTHER hesitates.

> I can help you disappear for as long as you want, or you can wait till that redneck hauls you home like a runaway pig. It's up to you.

ESTHER looks around the deck, finds a pencil and a scrap of paper, and starts writing. In the kitchen, ANTHEA shakes her head.

ANTHEA

> A knife. A KNIFE. I should be calling the police.

TODD

> Look – within his little pea brain, he was protecting her. If A.D. likes you, he will throw himself in front of a train for you. He's a loyal friend. A friend who sticks up for you no matter what.

Beat.

ANTHEA

> You're one to talk about friendship. You're the one who –

Beat.

> – ESTHER!

She moves toward the deck; TODD goes to intercept her.

> Get out of my way. Or are you going to fight me, too.

Beat. ANTHEA goes out onto the deck. ESTHER is gone.

ANTHEA
    Esther?

    TODD, moving onto the deck, finds ESTHER's note.

TODD
    (*reading aloud*) "Don't worry. I'm okay. I'm not telling you where I am."

ANTHEA
    Esther? ESTHER? ESTHER!

TODD
    ESTHER!

    SETH bursts in from the hall.

SETH
    I JUST BEEN TOWED.

Act I **Scene 5**

A few hours later. The subway station. ESTHER and A.D. run on, then double over, laughing like maniacs. ESTHER shows signs of a department store makeover. She is dressed in cheap and flashy mall gear – including a black Joan Jett wig – yet still sports her steel-toed boots and carries her John Deere cap in hand. Her clothes are covered in price tags. As their excited laughter subsides, A.D. looks back the way they came.

A.D.

We're clear. Probably lost that mall cop at the first set of stairs.

> *Beat.*

You look great.

ESTHER

Really?

A.D.

Oh, yeah. "High School Confidential" meets "Bad Reputation." Better ditch the tags before we get on the train.

> *He starts pulling the tags off the merchandise, breaking the plastic tethers with his hands. As he does so, ESTHER takes in the price tags ... and sobers up fast.*

Stand up.

> *She does, and he looks her up and down.*

Mm. Got to lose the boots, though; they scream "Take me home, I must milk the pigs." And don't get me started on this cap ...

> *ESTHER stares at him as if she hasn't seen him properly before.*

What?

ESTHER
    We stole.

A.D.
    Uh-huh.

ESTHER
    We ran.

A.D.
    With you so far.

ESTHER
    We scammed our way in here with some kind of weird coins I've never
    even seen before.

A.D.
    Pesos, pesetas, rupees, and rubles. The world comes here to dump its
    worthless crud. No offence.

ESTHER
    Gimme some potatoes.

        She pronounces it "puh-TAY-tuhs."

A.D.
    Pesetas … why?

ESTHER
    I'm calling Todd.

A.D.
    You crazy? What do you think we did this for? You go back to Todd's
    right now, what do you think is going to happen?

ESTHER
    I don't care. I'm not this – I'm not some little –

        She indicates her outfit.

    – whoever this is!

A.D.
    And that's why it's called a disguise. The cops'll –

ESTHER
    – Give me the money. Give me some fake money for the stupid pay phone
    or I'll call the police and turn myself in.

She stretches out her hand.

A.D.

Wow. Here you go, Princess. Pleasure doing business.

> *ANTHEA, at TODD's apartment, is on the phone with*
> *SETH, at a pay phone.*

SETH

Cost me a hundred bucks for the truck, and five for the cab ride. I'm goin'
home.

ANTHEA

She's not back yet.

SETH

She'll come back. She might not be ready to come home.

ANTHEA

I don't accept that.

SETH

You think I like it?

> *Beat.*

You figure things out here, I'll figure things out at the farm; come back
Sunday, pick you both up. I gotta go.

ANTHEA

Of all the people she could've gone to. After what he did …

SETH

She doesn't know what he did.

ANTHEA

I should tell her.

SETH

NO. She don't need to know!

ANTHEA

I should call the police.

SETH

There's no need to get our daughter mixed up with the police.

ANTHEA

We don't even know where she –

SETH

– I know my girl. She will come back in her own time. You bullied her
on church, she ran. Tried to bully her home, she ran. You can force a
thoroughbred onto a trailer, but somethin's gonna break.

ANTHEA

You coddle her, Seth. She needs our guidance. Loving her is not enough;
it's our duty to love her into the Kingdom.

SETH

It's our duty to look after her inheritance, too, and right now we're doin' a
piss-poor job of both! I got five thousand broilers almost ready to ship,
but if anything goes wrong and we're not there ... I got a mortgage went
from eight to twenty-two percent overnight, and if I miss the payments
one more time ... and if we do lose the farm, what do we feed her with,
Anthea? The loaves and the fishes? Anthea?

He realizes she has hung up. Beat.

Hold on. Dalzell land. God made us stewards of that land.

Beat. He puts down the phone.

Hold on ...

Back in the subway, A.D. is fidgeting with annoyance.
ESTHER returns, scowling, jingling the change in her hand.

ESTHER

Line's busy.

A.D.

What a coincidence. So am I.

He starts off.

ESTHER

WAIT! DON'T LEAVE ME HERE! PLEASE!

He stops.

A.D.

What?

Beat.

You want to go home so bad, go. You knock on Todd's door, I give it four minutes till you're headed back to Green Gables or whatever haystack you rode in from.

ESTHER
The train scares me.

A.D.
Look, if someone hassles you –

ESTHER
– No, the *train* scares me. Nothing comes at you that close that fast unless it wants to run you down. I feel like it's going to crush me. I feel like I'm going to fall.

A.D.
That's crazy.

ESTHER
I know.

A.D.
You're up here, on a platform. It's down there, on a track.

ESTHER
I know that!

    Beat.

You know what? I hate it here … too much, too many, too loud, too fast … like half the time I can't even understand what anyone's saying, maybe it's supposed to be English but it might as well be … Portuguese! There's people sleeping on the sidewalk – but you all whizz by them like they're dog poop with eyes! How can you live like this?

    Beat.

A.D.
So on the one hand, we're heartless bastards; on the other hand, we should all "talk White"?

ESTHER
That's not –

A.D.

– You want to hate this city, fine. But don't hate it cuz you're scared, cuz you don't get it, cuz you never really tried. That's lazy, Princess.

ESTHER

I am not –

A.D.

– If you crawl right back to the devil you know – when you left with the clothes on your back cuz that's how bad it sucked – then nothing's changed; you just gave up.

ESTHER

I am not –

A.D.

– Prove it. Spend one night in my world. Then go home, shoot a moose, fertilize your cabbage, whatever you people do for fun. At least you'll be making a choice, not running away.

She looks at him for a long moment.

ESTHER

One night. No stupid stuff. I've got nothing to prove to you.

A.D.

Now that's my girl ... or, "*uma boa menina.*" As we say in Portuguese.

ESTHER

You're Portuguese?

A.D.

Sure. Portuguese, Guyanese, Lebanese, you name it. A.D.: All-Dressed! I am a proud Mick Spic Flip Wop Wog Frog Chinko Faggot, and this city is my nation because I could not exist anywhere but here. So if you want to learn how to survive ...

A train approaches. He takes her by the collar and belt and shoves her up against the edge of the platform.

ESTHER

Wait ... WHAT ARE YOU DOING? LET ME GO!

A.D.

Get brave, Princess ... or get home.

As he holds ESTHER's collar and waistband firmly from behind, she feels the wind from the train.

A.D.
Breathe …

At first she is rigid with fear, but finally – as the last cars go by – she relaxes a little, and breathes.

Act I **Scene 6**

Early Saturday morning. Outside TODD's apartment.
ESTHER is bubbling over with happiness.

ESTHER

> ... and I want bacon, and sausages, and pancakes, and syrup. And poached eggs and cream of wheat and strawberry jam ...

A.D.

> Impressive. You're not even high.

ESTHER

> A giant painting in five kinds of pink! A twenty-minute drum solo on plastic buckets! Pepperoni pizza at three in the morning! Whatever people want, here, they just ... do it!

A.D.

> The look on your face when you finally figured out that woman was a hooker. So what gave it away, Princess? The six-inch red stilettos, her date dropped her off on the corner, or the neon sign over her head that said "I am a hooker"?

ESTHER

> You think I don't know anything because I'm a little farm girl? I've killed more stuff than you have. And I guarantee I've seen more ... willies than you have, too.

A.D.

> Okay, but have you ever put one in your –

ESTHER

> – Ever clean a horse's sheath?

A.D.

> A what?

ESTHER

A sheath.

A.D.

Like ... where you put a sword?

ESTHER

Kind of ... a male horse's, you know, thing ... it's ... retractable. Folds
into this ... pouch. Which gets filled with ... dirt and stuff. So you squirt
in some mineral oil and ... get him to ... let it all hang down. Then you
reach inside with a cloth covered in –

A.D.

– Oh my God. You've given a hand job to a horse?

ESTHER

No, that's not –

A.D.

– Wow. The night you break your chastity pledge, you are in for a world of
disappointment.

> She whacks him playfully and heads off toward the
> apartment. He hangs back.

ESTHER

Aren't you coming home for breakfast?

A.D.

Gonna grab something at the corner. I'll bet your daddy's in there waiting
for me with a pitchfork and a rabid chicken. See ya.

> Interior of an all-night coffee shop. ANTHEA is seated at a
> table with a cup of coffee. A.D. walks by.

ANTHEA

You're him. You're that boy!

A.D.

Oh, shit.

ANTHEA

Stop – please! I won't – I just want to find my daughter, I just want to
know she's all right! Have you seen her? Do you know where she is?

> Beat.

If you tell me where she is, I promise I won't … drag her home. I'll call off the police. I just … really want to talk to her. I'm her mother. Do you understand?

He nods.

So … where is she? Is she okay?

A.D.

She's fine. (*pointing down the street*) She's right there.

ANTHEA

At Todd's? No, she can't be. I sat right here all night, I have a perfect view of the front door.

A.D.

No one under thirty uses Todd's front door.

ANTHEA

I see.

Beat.

Will you please tell her I'll be here all day in this coffee shop, if she wants to come and talk? Could you do that?

He nods.

Todd told me your name, but it's gone right out of my head. What is your name?

A.D.

A.D. … for "Attention Deficit." Oh, look, a penny.

He makes for the door.

ANTHEA

WAIT! I'll buy you breakfast. Order anything you like.

A.D. hesitates. ANTHEA calls toward the counter.

Excuse me, may we have –

A.D.

(*calling toward the counter*) – the usual … With an extra-large coffee … and a Dutchie. To go.

He settles, as far away from the table as possible. Beat.

ANTHEA

So. What did the two of you do last night?

A.D.

What – aside from the heroin and turning tricks on Jarvis?

Beat.

Wow, they're not kidding about you Jesus freaks and your sense of humour.

Beat. He relents.

We consorted at a concert outside City Hall, and dancèd unto demon rock 'n' roll; we wanderèd down Queen Street and gazèd on graven images; we renderèd unto Pizza Pizza what was due unto Pizza Pizza. Then we watchèd the sun rise over the lake, and lo, we saw that it was good. Do I get my breakfast now?

Beat.

ANTHEA

What are you so afraid of, son?

A.D.

I dunno. Waking up in Utah with a bump on my head and three child brides named Jolene?

Beat.

What are you afraid of? Esther wakes up in some drummer's bed with a tattoo that says "Property of the Band"?

ANTHEA

Yes.

Beat.

A.D.

Okay, yeah, that could happen.

Beat.

One thing I know? If there is a God, he hates my guts. Cuz whenever someone tries to beat the shit out of me, they always talk about God.

ANTHEA

Those people are goons, son. I'm sorry.

Beat.

God doesn't hate you. He loves you very much. But He loves you like a father, a good father, the kind you deserved and never got. So sometimes He has to do what's best for you even if you don't like Him for it.

A.D. blinks at her for a moment, then goes on the attack.

A.D.

How can you believe every word in the Bible when you're only ever reading the translation? How can you seriously believe the world was created in six days? I can't even get rid of a zit in six days. And our creator would send us all to everlasting torture, except his son agreed to die a horrible death? How can you possibly worship someone like that?

ANTHEA

Who do you worship?

A.D.

Nobody. The universe is random. It starts with the Big Bang. The stars form into galaxies, some lady pops us out, we do the best we can, we die.

ANTHEA

Where did the Big Bang come from?

A.D.

What?

ANTHEA

If the universe is simply a collection of stuff expanding outwards from the Big Bang ... where did the Big Bang come from?

Slight pause.

Have you ever been in trouble, A.D.? Bad trouble, trouble where you thought you would never get out? Find yourself muttering, "Please, no ... please ... oh, please ..."

Beat.

Who do you think you were talking to?

Beat.

A.D.

Look. I think you should let her stay here with Todd for a while. He just has –

ANTHEA
   – all the answers –

A.D.
   – has a way of letting us figure things out. Esther … hasn't figured things out. Not yet.

ANTHEA
   Thank you for your concern, but my husband will be back tomorrow, and he's going to take us home.

A.D.
   Us? She ain't a-comin' home agin, Ma Walton. I'm giving you that much for free.

> *ESTHER is on the deck, curled up in a chair, when TODD appears, nursing a mug of tea. They look at each other.*

ESTHER
   Hi.

TODD
   Hi.

ESTHER
   Mom and Dad?

TODD
   Gone, for now.

> *Beat.*

   A.D.?

ESTHER
   Coffee shop.

> *Beat.*

   He thinks you're mad at him.

TODD
   Smart boy.

> *Beat.*

ESTHER

> He's been hovering over me all night. Like a cross between a chaperone and a German shepherd.

>> *Beat.*

> A shepherone.

>> *Beat.*

> He finally showed me some of his art! What an imagination! There's stuff all over the neighbourhood, he calls it "installations."

TODD

> Does he.

ESTHER

> Yeah! Cuz he installs it in places! Like a whole bus shelter that he turned into, like, this little apartment for Crazy Patty the bag lady, with this little tiny bed and a carpet and a mini-armchair ... he even made her portrait and hung it on the wall! And there's a sign outside that says "Homeless. Shelter." He wants to put them up all over the city, faster than the cops can take them down ... I want to help him ...

>> *Beat.*

> Todd? I'm ... sorry I ran out on you like that.

>> *Beat.*

TODD

> Why didn't you tell me you were Seth and Anthea's daughter?

>> *ESTHER looks at him, shrugs.*

> What have you heard about me?

ESTHER

> I heard ... this was a safe place to go. Simon Coyte told me, if a kid from home was in trouble, you wouldn't turn them away.

>> *Beat.*

TODD

> Anything else?

>> *Beat.*

ESTHER

Different things, I guess. Like, one time I found this photo in Grandma's album, "Christmas Dinner, 1955," and there was a boy next to Dad I didn't recognize. So I said to Grandma, "Who's this?" and she said, "That's Todd," and then she tore up the photo and cried.

Beat.

That was you, right? In the picture?

TODD

I don't know. I haven't seen the picture.

Beat.

ESTHER

So ... how'd you know my dad?

TODD

You should probably ask your dad.

ESTHER

You've got to be kidding. Like they'd ever tell me anything.

Beat.

Todd ... did, um, so, um ... why did you leave?

Beat.

I mean, it was a long time ago. Like before I was born.

TODD

Yes. It was a long time ago.

Beat.

ESTHER

Are you mad at me?

TODD

(*sighing*) No, Esther, I am not mad at you. It is not your fault that life, like a good Bordeaux, gets more complex with age ... do you want to go home?

She shrugs.

If you don't, then you need your parents' permission to stay ... or you need to go to court.

ESTHER
Don't want to talk to some judge.

TODD
Then we'll ask them to meet us somewhere.

ESTHER
Here.

TODD
On neutral ground. Do not use me to punish your parents, kiddo.

ESTHER
I'm not!

Beat.

Maybe a little.

Beat.

I feel strong here. It's hard to feel strong around my mother.

TODD
I know.

ESTHER
Unless A.D.'s there. I want A.D. to be there, too.

TODD
Uh-huh.

Beat.

Esther, I'm assuming it has not escaped your attention that I am a man
who likes men, i.e., a homo, a fruit, a friend of Dorothy. I am, in point of
fact, gay –

ESTHER
– I know –

TODD
– and so is A.D. You do know that, don't you?

Beat.

ESTHER
Well, yeah. Sure. Yeah. Sure. Of course I know that … so, are you, I mean,
are the two of you …

TODD

(*gently*) No, honey. We're basically family. And besides, my heart belongs to Burt Reynolds ...

A.D. appears at the top of the back stairs, with his hands up.

A.D.

I am turning myself in –

TODD

– into Lady Di? Because otherwise I'm not that interested.

A.D.

No, I'm serious, I'm sorry. I was an idiot. I coulda got us all in a lot of trouble. I'm gonna try to use my head for a while, see where that gets me.

Beat.

TODD

I should have called the cops on you myself. Could have spent one whole night without needing a defibrillator.

A.D.

You'd flatline from boredom. (*to ESTHER*) Your mom's in the coffee shop. Says she'll wait there all day.

ESTHER moans.

Hey. You can get through this, Princess. Promise.

Long beat. TODD looks up at the sky.

TODD

You know what I miss sometimes, from back home? I miss the morning star ... "How art thou fallen from heaven, O Lucifer, son of the morning!"

They look at him.

Isaiah. 14:12.

Act I **Scene 7**

Later the same Saturday. The coffee shop. ESTHER and ANTHEA sit across from each other, not drinking their coffee.

ESTHER
I want to stay.

ANTHEA
I'm sorry?

ESTHER
I don't want to go home.

ANTHEA
Well, we want you to come home.

ESTHER
A.D. was at this alternative school downtown. It sounds so great. I can finish high school here. A.D.'s grades were worse than mine are –

ANTHEA
– Your grades have always been –

ESTHER
– Not lately – and he turned it around and this fall he's going to art college.

Beat.

ANTHEA
You've thought this out.

ESTHER
Yeah.

ANTHEA
You've talked it over with Todd?

ESTHER
    Not exactly.

ANTHEA
    Who, then? A.D.?

ESTHER
    Yeah.

        Beat.

    I can start in the fall.

ANTHEA
    You have a little crush on this boy.

ESTHER
    Oh, brother –

ANTHEA
    – You do, don't you?

ESTHER
    Here we go. No, I do not have a –

ANTHEA
    – Now who do you think is going to pay for all this? Does A.D. have any
    ideas about that? Your father and I can't afford –

ESTHER
    – Yeah but I'll be turning sixteen so I can apply for student welfare.

ANTHEA
    Welfare? You want to go on welfare?!

ESTHER
    Student welfare, yeah. You don't even have to officially kick me out, you
    just have to sign something saying –

ANTHEA
    – that we can't support you –

ESTHER
    – or won't; whichever. And you just said you can't.

        Beat.

ANTHEA

You run away from home, you scare your father and me half to death, you start holing up with Todd Wishart, of all people ... and then you march in here, looking like – And now you want us to send you off to private school –

ESTHER

– alternative school –

ANTHEA

– as if you were the Queen of England! What do you expect me to say?

ESTHER

I'm not coming home with you, Mom. I'll stay here or ... I'll just ... go.

Pause. ANTHEA sighs.

ANTHEA

Come to church with me tomorrow. And we will pray on it.

ESTHER

Okay.

ANTHEA

You really hate it that much. At home. You are that miserable there.

ESTHER

Mom, I ... I'm not supposed to be there. That's all. I'm supposed to be here.

Act I **Scene 8**

Sunday, mid-morning. A.D. is on the deck. He has a little TV with him. As he watches a World Cup qualifying match, we hear tinny cheers and breathless announcements in Spanish. SETH appears on the deck. He sees A.D. and freezes. They look at each other warily.

SETH
You gonna pull another knife?

A.D.
It's Sunday.

SETH
"Angel of Death" gets a day off?

A.D.
Yep.

> *Beat.*

SETH
Esther not back from church yet?

> *A.D. shrugs. SETH's eyes focus on the game. He pulls a stick of beef jerky out of his pocket and offers it, offhandedly, to A.D.*

SETH
Jerky?

A.D.
I'm a vegetarian.

> *Beat. SETH chews his jerky.*

SETH

What in blazes are they jabberin' away in?

A.D.

Why do you care?

SETH looks him up and down, then looks away.

SETH

I don't recognize this city anymore. (*impatiently*) What's takin' them so long?

A.D.

It's your church. How long does it usually take for two thousand years' worth of abracadabra and spookity-woo?

Beat.

SETH

This must be your lucky day, son. My arms hurt.

SETH turns back to the television. Pause.

A vegetarian.

A.D.

Yep.

SETH

I figure all vegetarians are either crazy or stupid. Which are you?

A D

(*amiably*) Screw you, Archie Bunker.

SETH

No, I really want to know. I've never met a vegetarian before. So what's the matter with meat, anyway? Do you cry for the baby seals and all that?

A.D.

There's other things.

SETH

Like?

A.D.

Like, land use.

SETH

    Land use.

A.D.

    I read somewhere you get like ten times as much protein per acre off of beans as off of meat.

SETH

    Is that a fact.

A.D.

    Yep.

        Beat.

SETH

    I got fifty acres out back of my barns, soil's wrong for corn, wrong for anything'll turn a profit, ground's rocky as blazes, hills are that steep they'd tip my tractor onto my head if I was dumb enough to plough 'em. Woods. Streams. Bulrush swamps. You want me to take that good cattle land and grow tofu?

A.D.

    Soy.

        SETH snorts.

SETH

    Soy. You think I don't know what soy is, boy? I know what soy is. Soy's what you feed to hogs so they can turn it into food.

A.D.

    Maybe you shouldn't put anything on that land, then. Maybe you should let it go back to nature. Harvest the ... berries, or whatever. Or give it back to the Native people. It's theirs, anyways.

        As A.D. speaks, TODD comes into the kitchen, bearing a tray with two takeout coffees. TODD is about to come out to the deck, but stops when he sees SETH. Beat.

SETH

    Will you get this idiot out of my sight?

TODD

    Why are you here?

SETH

I am waitin' for my wife and daughter to get back from church so I can
drive them home.

TODD

A.D., you want to come in here a moment? I got coffee.

> *A.D. shuffles into the kitchen.*

You all right?

A.D.

Sure. A few minutes of my day, I'll probably never see him again, he can
say what he wants. (*shrugging*) Urban life.

> *Beat.*

I'm gonna go crash. Yell if you need backup.

> *He goes out with his coffee. TODD looks at the remaining
> coffee for a moment, hesitating. He finally peeks out onto
> the deck.*

TODD

(*stiffly*) Coffee?

SETH

(*stiffly*) Okay.

> *TODD comes out, warily. He leaves the coffee beside SETH,
> who seems to be watching the game. As TODD is going back
> inside, SETH speaks.*

Saturday night last night.

TODD

Yes. Yes, it was.

SETH

So how are the park washrooms these days? They clean the floors pretty
regular? Or do you run out of toilet paper?

TODD

Matter of fact, Seth, times have changed for us fairies. Some of us support
a vibrant bathhouse scene. Others have dates in actual restaurants. In fact,
I had one just the other night. Corner of You Don't Wanna Know and
Mind Your Own Business.

Beat.

And so long as I am keeping a roof over your daughter's head, you will shut your pie-hole about all that goes on in the bedrooms of the nation. My house, my rules.

SETH
(*very deliberately*) I'm not in your house.

> *The doorbell is heard. TODD goes out and comes back with ANTHEA, who is agitated and alone.*

ANTHEA
(*as they come in*) Where is she?

TODD
I thought she was with you.

ANTHEA
Have you seen her at all today?

TODD
No.

ANTHEA
What about A.D.?

TODD
I'll ask him.

ANTHEA
(*as TODD goes out*) Have you seen Seth?

SETH
Out here.

> *She moves to the doorway between the kitchen and the deck.*

ANTHEA
She didn't come to church. What did you say to her?

SETH
Haven't seen hide nor hair of her since Friday. What did you say to her?

> *TODD comes back; he shakes his head.*

ANTHEA
I'm calling the police.

SETH
    DON'T –

ANTHEA
    – OUR DAUGHTER IS MISSING! I DON'T HAVE TIME FOR YOUR
    ANYTHING-GOES, HANDS-OFF PARENTING! Honestly, Seth,
    sometimes I think we are unequally yoked. (to TODD) This is your fault.

TODD
    My fault?!

ANTHEA
    You're enjoying this, aren't you? You can finally have the last laugh on
    us all. "Hey, kids, try life in the Big City! All of the fun, none of the
    consequences!" You're the Pied Piper, taking our children to make us pay –

TODD
    – Except they come to me, Anthea. The ones that need to, they track me
    down. Believe me, I did not ask to be the Harriet Tubman of Baker's
    Creek. Now, someone is sleeping back there, so could both of you, please,
    go be afraid of Virginia Woolf somewhere else.

SETH
    What's he talkin' about?

TODD
    Oh, for the love of Judy, join the twentieth century before it's too late!

SETH
    (to ANTHEA) I'll be waitin' in the truck.

        SETH storms into the hall. We hear a door slam. ESTHER
        comes up the back stairs and into the kitchen. ANTHEA is
        on her like a dirty shirt.

ANTHEA
    You weren't at church.

ESTHER
    Good morning.

TODD
    Morning, honey.

ANTHEA
    You didn't come to church.

TODD

I don't know, Anthea, she's here now, maybe we could start from there?

ANTHEA

(*to TODD, with dazzling politeness*) Todd, could you give me a moment
alone with my daughter? Please. If you don't mind.

> *Beat.*

TODD

All right. But remember the house rules: no knives, no guns ...

> *He goes out onto the deck. Sits and stares into the distance.
> Meanwhile, ESTHER and ANTHEA square off in the
> kitchen.*

ANTHEA

You didn't go to church.

ESTHER

I don't want to go to church.

ANTHEA

There's a lot of things you don't want to do these days. But we don't do
what we please, in this family: we do what pleases God.

ESTHER

No, Mom, we do what pleases you. Or can you not tell the difference?

> *Beat.*

ANTHEA

What did you do with all your trip money, anyway? After we pinched and
scrimped ... what did you do with it?

> *ESTHER thrusts her hand into her pocket and hauls out its
> contents: a few crumpled bills and a handful of change.*

That's it? That's all that's left? Do you have any idea how hard it was
to make that money? You have no right to that money! You stole that
money! Now give it back!

ESTHER

I earned it. How much do you get for ten years of slave labour?

> *ANTHEA slaps ESTHER. Silence.*

ANTHEA

I look at you and I have no idea what I'm seeing. I hear you and think I must have had some kind of stroke. Who is this rude proud deceitful – when we have given you everything on a silver platter, everything we had, every possible, to be a good decent happy loving Christian. Not a brazen shameless … now unlike your father, unlike Todd, I don't have the luxury of being your friend. It is my job to "love you into the Kingdom," and that's exactly what I'm going to –

ESTHER

– You're right, Mom. You have no idea. I go to church and I see the same bunch of liars and coveters and gossips as everywhere else, except we're bigger hypocrites about it. School's a joke. Don't stand up, don't stand out, keep your head down, yes sir, no sir … make it to Saturday night, make out at Inspiration Point, go bombing down Swamp Road in a souped-up Camaro, wasted out of your mind –

ANTHEA

– Esther, are you … are you pregnant?

ESTHER

What?!

ANTHEA

Are you on drugs?

ESTHER

Mother, for once in your life, can you see what's actually going on?

Beat.

Back home it's a done deal. What I'm supposed to think. What I'm supposed to do. You've all got it all mapped out for me as far as the eye can see!

Beat.

I can finally be myself here. Whoever that is … and yeah, the air smells like garbage – but at least I can breathe. I can't breathe in your house.

ANTHEA

Esther, you are fifteen years old. Your home is with your mother and father, and we are breaking our backs to –

ESTHER

– Exactly! We break our backs, and for what? A "Century Farm." Who cares about a Century Farm? Farming is back-break work, stupid work … I'm not going to throw my life away on a stupid piece of dirt!

SETH has appeared in the doorway looking pale and holding his left arm.

ESTHER

(*shocked*) DAD!

TODD comes quietly back to the kitchen.

SETH

ESTHER … DON'T YOU – DON'T YOU WANT – MY ARM … HURTS –

ESTHER

– Dad, I'm sorry –

SETH hears an echo, a memory, and slumps over in pain.

TODD
  – Seth –
	FIRST BOY'S VOICE
	  Seth, I'm sorry!

ANTHEA Seth … what is it?	

SETH
  Don't touch me …
	SECOND BOY'S VOICE
	  Don't touch me, don't ever
	  touch me again!

SETH
  I think I'm gonna be sick …
	SECOND BOY'S VOICE
	  I think I'm gonna be sick …

TODD
  Seth, she didn't mean to –
	FIRST BOY'S VOICE
	  Seth, I didn't mean to –

SETH
  Abomination …
	SECOND BOY'S VOICE
	  You are an abomination to the
	  Lord, Todd Wishart, and you
	  will burn for all eternity!

TODD

You're white as a sheet …

SETH

TODD? WHY DO YOU TAKE EVERYTHING AWAY FROM ME?

TODD

You're sweating ...

SETH

My heart ... hurts ...

*He sways again, and collapses. TODD and ANTHEA rush
to help him; ESTHER remains frozen, apart.*

ANTHEA

Seth! SETH!

A.D. shuffles in.

A.D.

Okay, what is going on out here –

TODD

– A.D., call an ambulance. Seth is having a heart attack.

ESTHER looks on, helpless and alone.

End of Act I

Act II **Scene 1**

Sunday evening, one week later. As we return to our seats, TODD comes on and signals for attention.

TODD

Everybody, listen up: we're back. Hello? Everyone? That means you, too, Harvey. Harvey, in the immortal words of our dear Queen Mum: SHUTCHER PIE-HOLE!

Beat.

Thank you. Hope you all had a nice fifteen-minute break. The one that started half an hour ago.

Beat.

Listen, I do want to thank you all for coming to a committee meeting on a Sunday – when you could be watching *Hymn Sing.* You all know I'd rather stab myself in the eye than make an inspirational speech, but this past week I've been painfully reminded of coming to this city at seventeen: one more tragic fairy on the lam, lost, abandoned, and alone … I wish someone had been there for that idiotic, badly dressed, terrified kid, to tell him he was going to be okay … and that's what this community centre is about. We are a community now, darlings. Since no one's beating down the door to take care of us, we need to take care of ourselves.

Beat.

Because – in the sacred words of L'Oréal – we're worth it.

Beat.

Which brings me to our inaugural Pride cabaret fundraiser; and on that front, I have some very good news: Daniel & Daniel have agreed to do the catering; and our headliner will be Kitty-Kitty Bang-Bang in *La Cage aux Balls.*

Act II **Scene 2**

The Dalzell home. Wednesday, late afternoon. ESTHER comes in, dressed as she was at the beginning of the play: John Deere cap, plaid shirt, jeans, Grebs. She collapses onto a porch chair, staring up at the sky. After a few moments, we hear ANTHEA and SETH as they come toward the porch.

ANTHEA

(*off*) Seth, if you won't do as you're told, I will drive you right back to her office and you can take it up with her!

SETH

(*off*) Woman, you are crawlin' all over me like a flea in heat! Now give me a moment's peace or I will have another heart attack just to spite you!

    SETH shuffles into view.

SETH

Hi, Peanut.

ESTHER

Hi, Dad.

SETH

Everything okay out there?

ESTHER

Yep. What'd the doctor say?

ANTHEA

(*appearing*) She said he's recovering very well …

    SETH starts to go offstage but ANTHEA's voice stops him.

… but he is not to go out to those barns.

SETH

I been home a week now, I want to see my g.d. barns!

He passes his hand over his eyes. Beat.

I'll just put my head down for a minute first.

ANTHEA
You do that.

> *SETH shuffles into the house. ANTHEA turns to ESTHER.*

You done out there already?

ESTHER
Yep.

> *Beat.*

ANTHEA
Everything okay?

ESTHER
Yep. Barn alarm's still not working right. And I tried to fix the apron chain, but we'll have to unload the spreader by hand first …

ANTHEA
Well, your father can fix it … we just won't bother him with all of that yet. Everything okay with *you.*

> *ESTHER shrugs.*

Dinner's at five tonight. I need to talk to Pastor Glenn before Bible study, so we have to be out the door by six.

ESTHER
I'm not going.

> *Beat.*

You and Dad go ahead, I have to … fix that spreader …

ANTHEA
Esther, you don't want to miss this week … it's Jell-O Night! You love Jell-O Night! Right after Bible study, we're having the Jell-O–eating contest, Jell-O fights, and –

ESTHER
– The Jell-O slide?

ANTHEA

> They're putting plastic sheets down the hill this very minute (*as she goes into the kitchen*) ... and Michelle Thexton's back for the summer, you love Michelle ... and next week is Dutch Blitz ...

> *ANTHEA looks at the fridge, takes a small piece of paper from it, and storms back out with the paper in her hand.*

> Esther! When were you going to tell me the bank called?

ESTHER

> I put the message on the –

ANTHEA

> – And why did you pick up the phone? If I've told you once I've told you a thousand times, let it ring!

ESTHER

> Okay –

ANTHEA

> – Now, is this going in one ear and out the other? Because –

ESTHER

> – No, no, I just – I thought it might be for me.

ANTHEA

> You thought –

> *Beat.*

> Never mind. Dinner is at five. Be in the truck by six.

> *ANTHEA leaves. After a moment, ESTHER goes to the phone and dials. Then we see A.D., at his workplace, answer the ringing phone.*

A.D.

> Todd, I'm just finishing my shift, I will get cat food, I will take out the garbage, now will you please stop calling me and go on your damn date!

ESTHER

> A.D.?

A.D.

> Yeah? Wait ... Princess?

ESTHER
   Don't feel like one today.

A.D.
   S'wrong?

ESTHER
   Oh ... nothing ... I ... I really miss you ...

> *She cries. A.D. is at a loss.*

A.D.
   Hey, Princess ...

ESTHER
   Yeah?

A.D.
   How about I come out for a visit?

ESTHER
   What? When?

A.D.
   Uh –

A MAN'S VOICE
   (*off*) – A.D.! Come on, you little fag, I know you work here, I know you're
   in there! You think you could hide from me forever?

A.D.
   How 'bout right now?

ESTHER	A MAN'S VOICE
Are you serious? That would be so – I mean, Mom would – But you know what? I don't care. I –	I want my money, man. Where's my money?

A.D.
   – Yeah, yeah, that all sounds great. How do I get there, again?

ESTHER
   Dalzell Farm, Jericho Line, east of Baker's Creek. You can ask Todd –

A.D.
   – Never mind. I'll figure it out.

ESTHER
  A.D. ... thank you.

A.D.
  What are friends for.

A MAN'S VOICE
  Hey. Gayboy. I want my money. Hey. Kid. I'm not going anywhere ...

> *A.D. escapes, as we hear loud banging on the door.*
> *Meanwhile, ESTHER hangs up the phone at her end and*
> *practically dances upstairs. A moment later, SETH comes in.*
> *Stares at the phone. Picks it up and dials.*

SETH
  Wade?

> *Beat.*

Wade, it's Seth Dalzell –

> *Beat.*

– yeah – yeah – yeah.

> *Beat.*

I know that, Wade, but I thought it would be okay to – I mean, you're in
the phone book; we're in the same church, Wade – Anyway, I don't know
if you heard I just had a – Yes, thank you, I'm feelin' not too bad now –
Anyway, I thought you could explain to head office or what have you that
I need a little more time to make my payments for this month.

> *Beat.*

Okay, for last month, too ...

> *Beat.*

And the month before that. Now, lookit, head office didn't sell me that
tractor, John Deere didn't sell me that tractor, you did. And the haybine
and the round baler and the ... well now I got custom work for my baler,
I got buyers for my hay, and how am I supposed to get that hay without
a tractor and a baler and ... and I'm about to ship five thousand broilers,
this is where you get your money back, Wade, this is not the time to –

> *Beat.*

66

Well of course I've gotta pay the bank before I pay you, Wade, I gotta keep a roof over my family's heads – let those bank bastards jack up your mortgage to twenty-two percent overnight, see how you –

Beat.

Paid for, eh? Your whole house … good for you.

Beat.

No I won't, I won't call this number again – No, never mind, not to worry. Yep. Yep, you too, Wade, and hello to Mavis. Yep, see you Sunday.

He puts the phone down. Beat.

Lord, you know I'm not too good at prayin', but … it's bad this time, Lord. It's real bad.

Act II **Scene 3**

Thursday morning. Birdsong, the daytime calls of crickets.
A.D. is standing in the Dalzells' kitchen, tentatively, like a
burglar.

A.D.

(*loud whisper*) Princess?

> *He looks around, sees the figurine collection, and does a*
> *double take.*

Whoa. Red Rose. Are you guys, like, following me around? Is this *The Shining* or something?

> *He does the "redrum" finger gesture from* The Shining.

– Red Rose, Red Rose, Red –

> *ESTHER vaults in the window, making him jump.*

How long have you been waiting to do that.

ESTHER

My whole life.

A.D.

How's your dad?

ESTHER

Good. He's good. Doctor said to take it easy for a while …

A.D.

So you have to do his work, too? That's gotta suck.

ESTHER

I don't mind work.

A.D.

And your mom? Still out there stumpin' for the Lord? Did she haul you off to confession and stuff?

ESTHER
Confession's a Catholic thing. We're evangelical.

A.D.
We?

ESTHER
How's Todd?

>   *Beat.*

You did let him know you were coming, didn't you?

>   *Beat.*

Oh, A.D., you should tell him you're okay.

A.D.
Why? "He's not my mama, does he look like my mama –"

ESTHER
– Don't be a jerkwad. Call him tonight.

A.D.
Okay, okay –

ANTHEA
(*off*) Esther, I just heard on the radio there's a –

>   *ANTHEA comes in, wearing barn clothes. She catches sight*
>   *of A.D.*

A.D.
Hi … Mrs. D.

>   *Beat.*

ANTHEA
(*to A.D.*) What are you doing here? (*to ESTHER*) What is he doing here?

ESTHER
I –

ANTHEA
(*to ESTHER*) – Never mind. We need to get the cut hay off the south field. There's a storm due in tomorrow. (*to A.D.*) Think you can learn to drive a tractor?

A.D.

(*startled*) Uh … yeah?

ANTHEA

Good, then you can pull the hay wagon. I don't know if you can do a man's work, son. But we're about to find out.

And they're gone.

Act II **Scene 4**

*That night. A clear sky. The Dalzells' porch. A.D. and
ESTHER appear from the direction of the barns. They move
slowly, stiffly. ESTHER drops onto a chair, staring up into
the sky. Just as A.D. is about to plop down into a chair, he
stiffens, and swats. Swats again.*

A.D.

Uh, uh, AHHH! Why are there so many BUGS! The country is GROSS!
This whole farm is so full of freaky little flying BUGS, it's amazing there's
room left for, you know, air! When you brought sandwiches out to the
field, the flies went straight from drinking pus off a cow's eye to landing
on my food. The country SUCKS!

ESTHER

That squat you showed me had rats in it. And roaches.

A.D.

Roaches are easy. Step on 'em! Kill 'em with chalk! Rats run away if you
go –

He makes a horrible monster face.

– AAAHHHRRR ... flies go, "Eh, whatever" and fly up your nose!

He swats wildly about, in a Watusi of misery.

Motherf –

*ESTHER nonchalantly hands A.D. a can of bug spray. He
sprays himself frantically from head to toe, and the air
around him for good measure. He waits to check whether
the spray has had the desired effect; it has. At last, sighing
with relief, he sprawls into a chair and is still. For a moment.
Then he sniffs the air, follows the scent trail to his own sleeve,
and wrinkles his face in distaste.*

A.D.

    Okay, rain would've ruined the hay, I get that now. But did she really have to put me on a manure spreader, for two hours, shovelling –

ESTHER

    – manure –

A.D.

    – whatever – I mean, what crawled up her fundamentals and died?

ESTHER

    (*shrugging*) Spreader's broken.

A.D.

    Uh-huh.

        Beat.

    It never stops around here, does it?

ESTHER

    Nope.

        Beat.

    Hercules is bright tonight.

A.D.

    Her what?

ESTHER

    A.D., look up.

        He peers into the sky.

A.D.

    Whoa … where'd all that come from?

ESTHER

    They're called stars.

        Beat.

A.D.

    What gives?

ESTHER

    What?

A.D.
> With you! Since when did you get so comfortable here? "La-la-la, the
> stars in the sky, I love to work, we're evangelicals"! Where's my shopliftin',
> samosa-eatin' Joan Jett rebel?

ESTHER
> You know what? Practically the whole world is stuck where they don't
> want to be, doing stuff they don't want to do. That's the way it is.

A.D.
> You mean ... you're supposed to suffer? For the sins of the world? Didn't
> someone do that already?

> *Beat.*

ESTHER
> If I leave, Dad will die ... of a busted heart ... because I busted it.

A.D.
> Horseshit.

ESTHER
> Could you please not –

A.D.
> – You ran away to save yourself and Daddy had a heart attack. So now
> you're going to make everyone else happy: Daddy, Mommy, Jesus ...
> except it won't work, Princess: know why?

> *ESTHER, hearing a noise, puts a finger to A.D.'s lips, turns
> off the porch light, and the two of them shrink into the
> shadows. SETH comes downstairs and appears in the
> doorway. He looks around furtively, takes out a flask, and
> takes a long pull. More footsteps are heard on the stairs.
> SETH hurriedly hides his flask just as ANTHEA enters the
> kitchen.*

SETH
> Where is she?

ANTHEA
> Still in the barns.

> *Beat.*

SETH

You lettin' her hang around with that little punk?

ANTHEA

That little punk is surprisingly tough. We couldn't've got through today without him. Besides, Esther's witnessing to him. She's a good influence.

> *Beat.*

SETH

I'm thinkin' I should get Essie somethin' just for fun. Maybe a calf for 4-H.

> *Beat.*

ANTHEA

Seth. We're taking on water here … You saw it for yourself. I made more money substitute teaching last winter than the annual profit for this whole farm. How is that right?

SETH

Fine. I'll get a job, too.

ANTHEA

That's not the point … Esther's right: we are killing ourselves, and we can't even pay the interest on what we owe. We bid high and we're euchred and that's just the way it is.

SETH

You think it's my fault for expandin' the barns.

ANTHEA

We expanded the barns. Poultry seemed like the way to stay alive. I'm not blaming you.

SETH

All I wanted was a hutch for some hens. The banks were the ones sayin', "We're not gonna loan you a couple of grand for some little chicken coop. But if you want to build a barn for five thousand chickens …"

ANTHEA

I know.

SETH

Practically stuffed the money down my shirt.

ANTHEA

I know.

SETH

So now they should darn well help us out.

ANTHEA

That's not how it works.

SETH

All these old-timers with their cash in a mattress, too cheap to take a
chance. Laughin' at me. Be laughin' even harder now.

ANTHEA

I don't care what the neighbours think anymore. I'm tired.

SETH

You think I'm not?

ANTHEA

Is everything a contest with you? I'm tired!

> *Beat. She produces a sealed envelope and shows it to SETH.*

Farm Credit must've come by while we were out. Left this in the door.

SETH

What is it?

ANTHEA

You know what it is.

> *Beat.*

I was hoping … I thought, if we finally had it laid out in front of us, you'd
agree we're better off walking away. I wanted it to be your choice.

SETH

My choice.

ANTHEA

It's still your farm.

SETH

That's right. My farm. My father's farm, my grandfather's farm, my great-
grandfather's farm. There's a hundred years of Dalzell sweat in every
furrow of every field –

ANTHEA

– My sweat, too –

SETH

(*irritably*) – You know, half the time they only want you to talk to them, the banks, tell 'em what's goin' on. I never shoulda let you stop answering the phone.

> *Pause. Suddenly, ANTHEA moves closer to SETH and touches him – a simple gesture of tenderness.*

ANTHEA

Storm's still not here yet. The stars are so bright tonight ... you remember the first time we got to use the telescope at Camp Galilee? The first year you brought Todd, remember? Can you believe that was twenty-five years ago ... we were all so young ... you, me, and Todd, sneaking out of the cabins and meeting down by the lake and ... talking! So many things we were going to do. Mission work. Travel to the Holy Land.

SETH

(*shrugging*) Kids dream.

ANTHEA

The Hawthornes built a school in Tegucigalpa ... last year, Arthena Might lit a candle in Jerusalem. Baker's Creek people go places these days. Why not us?

SETH

This is Dalzell land. The land of my fathers.

ANTHEA

Now it's your land, Seth, and what good is it if you're six feet under it?

> *Beat.*

I could teach full time. Summers off! You know the Yellowlees boys are buying up land like crazy, and their hog operation needs a manager. We can do God's work and see the world just like we always wanted!

SETH

What about Esther? Where does she fit into your master plan?

ANTHEA

Honey, God doesn't care if Esther lives on this farm; God only wants her to live a good life.

SETH

Well, aren't I a lucky bugger to have a wife with a direct line to God.

> *He grabs the sealed envelope and destroys it.*

ANTHEA
> SETH!

SETH
> This farm is Esther's birthright. It belongs to her. Not the bank, not the
> government, not those maggots the Yellowlees boys gettin' fat on the
> death of farms. And the Devil will play shinny in hell before I let you
> sell it out from under her, to go and preach in some godforsaken jungle.
> Tegucigalpa ...
>
> > *Beat.*
>
> You never should've broke up with Todd. You could've saved his soul;
> then you both could've saved the world. Instead you're stuck with me and
> Esther. Dalzells. Right to the end.
>
> > *He stomps over to the back door and throws on his boots.*
>
> Do NOT come after me. I am sleepin' in the loft.
>
> > *SETH stomps out past the porch, slamming the door.*
> > *ANTHEA stares helplessly after him, then retreats back*
> > *upstairs. As A.D. and ESTHER slink back into the shadows,*
> > *SETH pulls out his mickey and raises it to his lips. Seeing*
> > *this, ESTHER involuntarily puts her hand over her mouth,*
> > *and the movement catches SETH's eye. He turns, and he*
> > *and ESTHER stare at each other for a long moment. Then*
> > *he tilts his head back and drains the liquor dry.*

SETH
> (*to ESTHER*) Time to grow up.
>
> > *As SETH stumbles off toward the barn, ESTHER holds on to*
> > *A.D. for dear life.*

Act II **Scene 5**

*Late Saturday afternoon. The Dalzell house seems deserted,
except by the ever-present sounds of bird and frog and
insect life and the occasional distant moo. TODD enters. He
pauses on the porch steps. He looks around, reshaping the
landscape of memory in light of current fact. Then he knocks
on the porch door. After a moment, ANTHEA comes down
the stairs. She is stunned to see TODD in the doorway.*

TODD
Hello.

ANTHEA
Oh … hello.

> *Beat.*

TODD
I got A.D.'s message on my machine a few days ago … that he was here …
I kept trying to call but … no one ever answers the phone.

> *Beat.*

How's … Seth?

ANTHEA
He's doing all right. Thank you. Resting.

TODD
Good.

> *Beat.*

Never thought I'd see this place again. Mrs. Dalzell's kitchen …

ANTHEA
My kitchen now.

TODD

> (*nodding*) Now you're Mrs. Dalzell.

> *Beat.*

> So, is A.D. around, or …

ANTHEA

> Oh. You've come to take him home?

> *TODD nods.*

> They're out in the barns, should be back any minute. I was about to put supper on.

> *Beat.*

TODD

> Thanks, we'll grab a burger on the way, at Southey's or something.

ANTHEA

> Southey's? Oh, they closed years ago. Years ago. There's a truck stop down the highway if you don't mind your burgers with a bit of sand … Splitrail Café's still around, you'd probably know everyone there.

TODD

> I probably would.

> *Excruciating beat. A.D. and ESTHER come in from the barn. A.D. is wearing overalls, rubber boots, and a plaid shirt. TODD is momentarily speechless. ANTHEA starts setting up for supper, moving back and forth between the fridge, kitchen, and pantry, which she continues to do under the following.*

A.D.

> (*calling*) Okay, Mrs. D, we finished the barns already, we're gonna go wash up.

> *He sees TODD.*

> Oh, hey.

ESTHER

> TODD!

> *She runs over to TODD and gives him a big hug.*

TODD

Hello, dear. My, don't you smell agricultural.

ESTHER

Back in a sec.

She runs into the hall. TODD and A.D. look at each other.

A.D.

What're you doing here.

TODD

The night you left, a gentleman named "Meathook" came looking for you. Said he'd already tried you at work. The cats and I couldn't help him. The hungry, hungry cats.

Beat.

Turns out his parole officer wanted to see him just as much as he wanted to see you. So *you* can tell me the rest of the story on the way home.

A.D.

I can't go right now, man, they need me.

ESTHER comes back in, drying her hands.

ESTHER

What? You're not –

TODD

– Your job needs you, too.

A.D.

They'll get someone else.

TODD

Exactly. And then how are you going to earn your tuition? In a rutabaga patch?

A.D.

I'm not ready to go, Todd.

TODD

A.D. ...

ESTHER

Mom ...

ANTHEA

> (*stiffly*) Todd ... you should have some supper, at least. I'm only doing chicken and cold salads. That's all anyone wants to eat these days.

> *Beat.*

> Please, join us. After all you've done.

A.D.

> (*quickly*) If you insist ... Ma'am ... I'll go wash up.

TODD

> (*quietly*) "Ma'am?" You must be hungry.

A.D.

> (*quietly*) She does this thing with potato salad, you'll cry like a baby.

> *ANTHEA calls upstairs.*

ANTHEA

> SETH! Soup's on! (*to ESTHER*) Go tell your father we have company.

ESTHER

> Yes, Mom.

> *She and A.D. go offstage. In laying the rest of the supper things out, TODD and ANTHEA work together, which they do surprisingly well. SETH comes and stands at the doorway, watching them. Then TODD sees him.*

SETH

> Evenin'.

TODD

> Evening.

SETH

> Somethin' to drink?

TODD

> Uh ... no, thanks, I'm driving.

ANTHEA

> Todd and A.D. are leaving after dinner.

SETH

> Lemonade? Anything stronger spoils the flavour of my medications.

TODD

Oh … yes, please.

ANTHEA

Help yourselves, everyone. We'll eat on the porch.

> *Meanwhile, SETH is pouring out two glasses of lemonade.*
> *He hands one to TODD and begins to take his pills. A.D.*
> *and ESTHER return, and they all serve themselves from*
> *various bowls and plates and file out to sit on the porch.*
> *They are about to start eating when ANTHEA speaks again.*

ANTHEA

Esther, would you please say grace.

> *ESTHER hesitates, but ANTHEA firmly grasps hands*
> *with her neighbours and everyone follows suit. To A.D.'s*
> *astonishment TODD also bows his head.*

ESTHER

Thank you for our food. And our friends. And our family.

EVERYONE BUT A.D.

Amen.

> *They begin to eat. Slight pause.*

SETH

Good potato salad, Anthea.

ANTHEA

Thank you, Seth.

> *Beat.*

I used low-fat yogourt, and extra mustard pickles for flavour; I hope you don't miss the mayonnaise.

SETH

It's real, real good.

TODD

Delicious.

ESTHER

Yeah, Mom. Thanks.

Slight pause.

ANTHEA
So, A.D. … you're starting college.

A.D.
Yeah, in the fall. Just art college.

ESTHER
He's really talented.

A.D.
I never would've made it if Todd hadn't got me into this alternative
school downtown. First school I ever saw that wasn't filled with Nazis and
morons.

TODD
And, fortunately for you, they don't mind if you come in through the
window.

ESTHER laughs. Slight pause.

A.D.
Hey, Mr. D. About your heart attack.

SETH
What about it?

A.D.
Well, must've been scary for you, eh? Falling on the floor and everything.
Did you think you'd been "slain in the spirit"?

SETH says nothing; A.D. sees the others looking at him.

What? I've been reading.

ANTHEA
Dear, we don't get "slain in the spirit" in our church.

A.D.
But you're, like, evangelists, right? I thought you were into that stuff.
Getting saved on TV … proclaiming the Rapture … shrieking in tongues
… you know, the full Billy Graham.

TODD
This is my fault. I never should've let you off the Ritalin.

ANTHEA
No, it's all right, A – May I ask you, dear, what is your Christian name?

Beat.

A.D.
Salvatore.

ANTHEA
How lovely. Well then, Salvatore, we conservative Christians are not all the same. In our church, we believe that speaking in tongues ended in Bible times … and salvation is constantly prayed for and struggled for – not handed out on television. You see, God's plan for us is recorded in His Book –

TODD
– Yes, Salvatore. His Book which says that you are an abomination.

ANTHEA
Scripture does not call you an abomination, Salvatore. Scripture says … certain … things … are off limits. For everyone.

TODD
Things like shrimp.

ANTHEA
Certain acts. Certain acts are abomination, that's all –

TODD
– So you love the sinner, even as you hate the sin?

ANTHEA
Yes –

TODD
– Oh, that makes me feel so much better. You don't hate homosexuals, as long as we don't do anything, you know, gay.

ANTHEA
(flaring) Todd, I am doing everything I can to show respect for you as a person, whatever your … lifestyle. Could you not show an ounce of respect for my beliefs?

TODD
Anthea. This is not a "lifestyle," this is who I am. Show some respect for that.

ANTHEA

I'm sorry, but God told us the way, the one way, to live a righteous life. And every time we look at His commands and say: "Just this once," or "God may have said that but He couldn't have meant it," we move further into darkness, and it gets harder to get where we need to go.

TODD

The map, huh?

ANTHEA

Yes, the map.

TODD

Tell me: in a fantastically complex universe, in a world with billions of life forms, in a species with room for Verdi and the Village People … why would God provide only one map?

ANTHEA

Because it's a map, Todd, not a list of suggestions! Maps are about facts, and the central fact is this: "I am the way, the truth, and the life: no man cometh unto the Father but by me"! And you knew that! You were halfway to the ministry, Todd. When you turned your back on God, you knew exactly what you were doing!

> *Beat.*

SETH

Well I'd say supper is done. Esther, why don't you take your friend inside and do the dishes for your mother.

ESTHER

Yes, Dad.

ANTHEA

If you two wash up, I'll take care of the barns.

> *She goes. A.D. and ESTHER clear the dishes to the kitchen, leaving TODD and SETH on the porch.*

TODD

We need to talk.

SETH

Leave me alone.

TODD

I left you alone for twenty-five years. It didn't help. Talk to me.

SETH

Go to hell.

He goes to leave. TODD puts a hand on his arm.

TODD

Seth ...

SETH whips TODD's hand away.

SETH

Don't you touch me!

TODD shoves SETH.

TODD

What is wrong with you?

SETH shoves back.

SETH

You. You're what's wrong with me. You, and your pansy friend!

They are shoving each other now. SETH escalates; however, TODD is a better fighter than SETH and quickly gains the upper hand, restraining SETH until he stops flailing.

TODD

What is wrong with you, you maniac!

SETH

Leave me alone, you faggot! Stay away from my wife! Stay away from my kid! I don't know why you've still got it in for me: you're the one who forced yourself on me in that change room, not the other way around!

TODD throws SETH off.

TODD

Forced myself?! Oh, get a grip. I kissed you. Once. And for that, I was Todd the Apostate, Todd the Fag, and I paid and paid and paid –

SETH

– What about me? I can never trust anybody like I trusted you. I brought
you into my church. I brought you into my family. We were like brothers,
and you betrayed me.

TODD

I betrayed …? You dumb son of a bitch, YOU BETRAYED ME!

> *Beat.*

We won the game; my head was a helium balloon. I tried to kiss you.
Okay? I'm sorry. But you … you didn't talk it out, or punch me, you just
took off and told – and the story got bigger and bigger – by the time it got
to church, I think I'd jumped the whole team in the showers. You blabbed
my secret to your mother … to my mother … to Anthea … I lost my
home, my church, and my two best friends at the age of seventeen. That's
one hell of a reckoning for one impetuous kiss.

> *They look at each other, panting. In the kitchen, ESTHER
> and A.D. are putting food away, scraping plates.*

A.D.

Your mom and Todd in the old days, I thought that was a shocker, but …
Todd was going to be a minister?! Isn't any of this blowing your mind?!

ESTHER

What is wrong with her?

A.D.

Huh?

ESTHER

How could she say that? About you and Todd?

> *A.D. helps himself to more potato salad.*

A.D.

What, the abomination thing? Or the part where we're going to hell?

ESTHER

How can you be so calm about it?

A.D.

(*shrugs*) People have been threatening me with hell my whole life,
Princess. And none of them ever made me potato salad.

Beat.

Anyways, you've been a Christian your whole life. What did you think you believed?

ESTHER

Not that. Church drives me crazy sometimes but ... but Jesus can't be about what she says he's about, or ... Jesus can't have gone through what he went through so you would go to hell. It can't come down to that.

Beat.

I can't do this. I can't be here right now.

Beat.

I have to go.

A.D.

Huh?

ESTHER

Right now, to ... things I love. Things that aren't ... complicated ... come with me.

A.D.

Where?

ESTHER

You'll see.

She climbs into the window frame, holding out her hand.

A.D., I need you.

A.D.

Good enough for me.

As they climb out together, A.D., on an impulse, turns back ... to grab the bowl of potato salad. Then they are gone. On the porch, SETH looks over at TODD.

SETH

MAYBE THAT'S IT. MAYBE THAT'S WHAT I SHOULD DO.

Beat.

TELL THE TRUTH. BE A MAN. TAKE THE CONSEQUENCES.

(*to TODD*) We're losin' the farm. She always loved you. I have lost all hope that God will save me.

> *Beat.*

NOPE. THAT DON'T HELP ME ONE LITTLE BIT.

TODD
Then stop.

SETH
One more.

> *He and TODD look at each other.*

I miss my friend.

Act II **Scene 6**

*Early Sunday morning. Thunder and rain. Some
contemporary Christian music comes up – perhaps
something sweet and melodic by Keith Green, like "Open
Your Eyes." A.D. and ESTHER are up in her room. There is a
portable cassette player connected to headphones, which are
connected to A.D., who is listening to something we can only
faintly hear. He rips the headphones off.*

A.D.

Don't take this the wrong way, okay? Tonight was a blast. Midnight trip
through the woods ... skinny-dipping ... massive thunderstorm ... whoa.
But ... "Christian rock"? Like getting scratched to death by kittens while
Pat Boone pounds a spike through my head.

ESTHER

You don't like it.

A.D.

I wouldn't say that. I hate its sexless guts. That's what I'd say.

ESTHER

It's not supposed to be turned toward sex. It's supposed to be turned
toward God. That's the point.

A.D.

There's only one "point" rock music is turned toward, Princess ...

ESTHER

Why do you have to be such a jerk. I'm trying to share something really
important to me –

A.D.

– I told you –

ESTHER
> – Yeah, your daddy kicked you out and it's all Jesus's fault. Is that your excuse for everything?

A.D.
> Screw you.

> *He heads for the door.*

ESTHER
> Why do you have to be so vulgar all the time?

A.D.
> Because I damn well feel like it. Oh, am I supposed to tiptoe round your virgin ears … Saint-Esther-of-the-Manure-Pile? I came to save you from all that Jesus People garbage – and now you lay this on me. One minute you're done being a country bumpkin, the next minute you're all Back to the Land. You're done, you're back, you're done, you're back, hand me a scorecard, I can't keep up.

ESTHER
> You know what? You're an ignorant bigot and I'm not putting up with it any more.

A.D.
> I'm a bigot?!

ESTHER
> You think all Christians are country, and everyone country is Christian, and all of us are idiots. That's ignorant. So what if there's six churches in Baker's Creek: some people don't go to any of them, and why's there six churches if we're all the same? Plus, if we lived in some village in India or something, then that would be all cool, and you would talk all nice, no matter if you agreed with me or not. Well guess what. I could say Christians built this country. I could say city people are useless as tits on a boar. I could say that, but I don't.

> *ANTHEA, in barn clothes, comes into their space.*

ANTHEA
> You're awake. Time to do the chores.

ESTHER
> In a minute.

ANTHEA
You do the poultry, I'll do everything else.

ESTHER
In a minute.

> *Beat.*

ANTHEA
We're leaving for church at 8:45. A.D., you're welcome to come.

> *Beat.*

A.D.
Thanks.

> *ANTHEA goes.*

ESTHER
Please tell me I'm not turning into her.

A.D.
You were a little scary there for a moment.

ESTHER
Sorry ...

A.D.
Actually, I ... I like your mom.

ESTHER
What?

A.D.
I know it's wacky, but ... I kind of like your mom.

ESTHER
My mother thinks you're going to hell.

A.D.
Yeah, but ... in this life, she's been nothing but nice to me. And it's not like she made the rules ... plus, she's always feeding me. The other night, we had pie.

> *Beat.*

ESTHER
You are so weird.

A.D.
I know you are but what am I?

Beat.

ESTHER
I want to play you something … different. It's … I don't know what you call it, exactly … but I like it.

As ESTHER puts a cassette in the player, A.D. idly picks up the case, glances at it … and stops dead.

A.D.
Where'd you get this? This album just hit the gay scene and we get everything first.

Beat. He points at a track listing.

They wrote this song for us.

ESTHER
He wrote it for his mother. It's a Christian band.

A.D.
The album's called *Boy*, there's a song called "Stories for Boys," the cover's a shirtless boy. Work it out.

ESTHER
You mean, that kid is supposed to be … attractive, or something? That's disturbing.

A.D.
Oh, grow up, I am so sick of that straight-people crap. I don't want to make out with that kid, I want to *be* that kid. He's … so … complete.

Beat.

There's nothing Christian in this music.

ESTHER
It's turned toward God. Listen.

She puts the headphones on A.D. and herself, and presses Play. They listen for a moment, and their heads begin to bob along to what will sound to us like a small tinny squawk.

A.D.

HEY.

ESTHER

WHAT.

> *Beat.*

A.D.

I NEVER HAD A SISTER BEFORE.

> *Beat.*

ESTHER

ME NEITHER.

> *The sounds of U2's "I Will Follow," from their 1980 album Boy, come up full. On the porch, TODD and SETH have blankets and coats drawn up around them, and are a few bottles down. Perhaps a soft rain is falling.*

SETH

I liked you. So if you're ... one of them, what does that make me?

TODD

A jackass, same as always.

SETH

Does that make me what you are?

TODD

How should I know? (*seeing SETH's distress*) Oh, look. We were seventeen. Who knows what all we were thinking back then. When you're seventeen in Baker's Creek, even the organist looks pretty hot.

SETH

Miss Pritchard? No, she doesn't.

TODD

Okay, maybe not Miss Pritchard.

SETH

That woman scares me.

TODD

Bad example. What I'm saying is, it was a long time ago and we were very, very young. Want to kiss me?

SETH

    What?

TODD

    When you look at me, right now, do you want to kiss me?

SETH

    (*considering TODD*) Go jump in the lake, you hairy old buggerlugs.

TODD

    Exactly. So then what's the problem.

        Beat.

SETH

    You want to kiss me?

TODD

    (*considering SETH*) Don't think so. You were a handsome lad, once, but … you haven't aged well.

SETH

    Neither've you.

TODD

    We're probably safe, then.

SETH

    Here's to that.

        They drink.

    You broke their hearts, you know. My mom and dad.

TODD

    They broke my heart, too.

SETH

    Mom, to her dyin' day, she always thought you would come back. Repent your sin. And all would be forgiven. But you chose your "lifestyle." And don't give me some bull how life is unfair for people like you; we all want things we can't have. It don't matter what you think about at night. It only matters what you do.

        Pause.

TODD

    You remember that Northern Nights tournament back in '56?

SETH

    The Manitowabi brothers –

TODD

    – The Manitowabi brothers –

SETH

    – Tough –

TODD

    – Tough as nails –

      Points to his chin.

    – Still got that scar –

SETH

    – Yeah, you shouldn't a' cross-checked him though –

TODD

    – He started it, the big bugger. But I guess his brothers finished it.

      Beat.

    Ran into one of 'em a while back. The little one.

SETH

    Kevin.

TODD

    Kevin Manitowabi. At a training seminar for volunteer youth counsellors. He was running it. Where's your brothers, I said: I want payback. Dead, he said. All dead. Suicide … booze … Kevin almost drowned himself in aftershave before he was done …

SETH

    (*whistles*) Poor Kevin.

TODD

    Then one day he's taking flowers to his family's graves. And he remembers how he and his brothers got put in a school where if you talked Indian or acted Indian, they'd punish you. "God will love you: all you have to do is choose to not be an Indian." So he stands by those graves with his flowers in his hand and he looks up at the sky and says, "I don't know about God's plan no more: good or bad, right or wrong … I only know one thing: I am an Indian. So let's start with that."

      Pause.

SETH

Why're you goin' on about Indians.

TODD

Oh, for Pete's sake, Seth, it's a metaphor –

SETH

– Don't you know enough to call them "Canada's First Nations"?

Beat. TODD grins.

TODD

Up yours, dumb-ass –

SETH

– You'd like that, fairy boy –

TODD

– You ignorant, inbred, xenophobic, homophobic, Tory-votin', rifle-totin', Bible-thumpin' hick.

SETH

(*toasting him*) You limp-wristed son of a bitch.

Sunday. A few hours later. In the church.

ANTHEA

When did Our Lord become human?

Beat.

I'll tell you when He became human. Not when He was born. Not when He died. No. Matthew 27:46: "*Eli, Eli, lama sabachthani?*" or "My God, my God, why hast Thou forsaken me?" Jesus comes to earth to take on human life and human death ... but in that moment He feels the Godhead in Him dying ... and is so profoundly alone ... can you imagine what it meant, for someone who experienced the Divine more fully and constantly than anyone who has ever walked this earth ... to be cut off from it altogether? Living on in body, even for a second, without that connection, that sustenance, that hope. The horror. The emptiness.

Beat.

You have no idea what I'm talking about, do you?

She looks around for several moments.

Kids, let's have a song. Let's have "Jesus Loves the Little Children." I need to hear your little voices. I just … really want to hear them now.

A group of youngsters, untrained, joyous, sings "Jesus Loves the Little Children."

Jesus loves the little children,
All the children of the world
Red and yellow, black and white,
They are precious in His sight.
Jesus loves the little children of the world …

Act II **Scene 7**

Sunday. Midday. The rain has stopped. SETH, on the porch,
wakes with a start. He looks around. No sign of TODD. No
sign of anyone. SETH feels his head and sits back, closing
his eyes. TODD comes down the stairs into the kitchen.
He looks like death warmed over. Glancing around to see
if anyone is watching, he takes his chequebook out of his
pocket and, sitting down at the kitchen table, begins to write.
SETH comes to the kitchen doorway and notices TODD
tearing off a cheque.

SETH

What's that?

TODD

Good morning to you, too.

    Beat.

It's exactly what it looks like: a rather large cheque. Do you have a
toothbrush? Aspirin? Possibly a guillotine?

SETH

What for?

TODD

My head, what do you think. Oh, the cheque … to help you pay down a
little bit of debt. Give you some breathing room, until you get back on
your feet. How about some coffee, can you point me toward some coffee,
at least?

    Beat.

You're my oldest friends.

    Beat.

Don't get too excited. It's a loan.

Beat.

SETH
I can't …

He goes onto the porch. TODD follows him.

TODD
Seth. This is a Century Farm.

Beat.

Let me help you stay on it a little longer.

A.D. and ESTHER enter.

ESTHER
Dad! Dad! Hey, Todd!

TODD
Hi, honey.

ESTHER
So, this morning I took A.D. to the Splitrail for pancakes –

A.D.
– Yeah, we found an extra bike in your loft. Man, it needs a tune-up –

ESTHER
– And it was like everyone in Catlow County was there …

A.D.
(*to SETH*) Mr. D., everyone was talking about you. Well, after they finished staring at me …

ESTHER
Everyone was saying how awful things are, farmers getting driven off their land … (*softly*) Dad … everyone knows the bank guy drove up here with a letter. Everyone knows that car.

Beat.

Old Mr. Cochrane was pounding his fist on the table about interest rates and tax relief and Vern Yellowlees was organizing people to come here and start hiding our equipment – the baler, the haybine … he says there's barns all over this county where bailiffs will never find them.

Meanwhile, ANTHEA appears from the direction of the driveway, still dressed for church.

ANTHEA
Hello. Everyone.

ESTHER
Mom, wait'll we tell you –

SETH thrusts TODD's cheque at ANTHEA.

SETH
– Look.

ANTHEA looks at the cheque. She takes it in.

ANTHEA
Oh, Todd … are you sure … no, we can't …

TODD
La-la-la, I can't hear you, it's a loan. Plus, happy birthday for the next hundred years.

ANTHEA throws her arms around TODD, giving him a quick kiss.

ANTHEA
(*heading into the kitchen*) You know what? We should celebrate. I've got pie in the pantry and grape Freshie in the fridge.

A.D.
Pie? This is a great day. (*following ANTHEA into the kitchen*) Hey, Mrs. D. … can I have mine with ice cream? Please?

ANTHEA
Of course you can, dear.

ESTHER
Todd, can you and A.D. stay for one more night?

TODD
Well … we'll have to see what your parents say …

ESTHER
Oh, they'll be fine with it. Right, Dad? (*to A.D.*) Tonight after supper, I want to play you some Larry Norman. Maybe some Resurrection Band.

A.D.
> More Christian rock? Yay.

>> *Meanwhile, ANTHEA opens the fridge ... and frowns. She opens the freezer. In both cases, there is no light, no sound. Perhaps liquid from the freezer splashes on her shoe. She sways for a moment.*

> Mrs. D., what's wrong?

>> *ANTHEA recovers and launches herself around the kitchen, flipping switches: nothing works. She disappears into the hallway for a moment, then sprints back out to the porch.*

ANTHEA
> *(to ESTHER)* Did you look in on the chickens?

ESTHER
> Oh geez, Mother, I'll go right now –

ANTHEA
> – How long has the power been out?

>> *Beat.*

> HOW LONG?

>> *They look at each other, confused. ANTHEA dashes out toward the barns. Suddenly, ESTHER gasps. She looks at SETH, but he is staring into the distance. She dashes out after ANTHEA.*

ESTHER
> MOM?

A.D.
> Esther? What the – what's going on?

SETH
> *(very matter-of-fact)* The poultry barn. It's all on electric now. Feed, water ... vents for the air. The air so the birds can breathe ...

TODD
> A.D., how long has it been since someone opened the door to that barn?

SETH

I should've fixed that barn alarm. The Lord helps those who help themselves.

TODD

(*to A.D.*) Go help Anthea. Do whatever she tells you.

A.D.

Aren't you –

TODD

– No. Go.

> *A.D. races off toward the barn.*

Seth. Seth, are you okay.

SETH

Sure has been a beautiful summer. Couldn't ask for a brighter sun or a softer rain.

> *Beat.*

The Lord had a fondness for fishermen, all right. Wonder why none of his apostles were farmers …

> *ANTHEA comes in slowly. TODD looks at her inquiringly; she shakes her head, unable to speak.*

SETH

All dead?

ANTHEA

All.

> *ESTHER enters, looking dazed and numb, supported by A.D. Silence. TODD shakes his head as if to clear it.*

TODD

All right. Someone needs to call the insurance company. Esther, do you know where they keep the policy.

> *ESTHER shakes her head. ANTHEA also shakes hers and raises her hand to signal TODD to stop. TODD understands. Absolute dead-stop silence. SETH gets up and goes down the porch steps. He kneels down on the ground and motions ESTHER over to join him. He picks up a handful of dirt, and*

lets it run through his fingers. Then he takes her hand, pours the dirt into it, and repeats the process.

SETH

You're right, Esther. Sooner or later it all comes down to dirt.

ESTHER

Dad ... Dad, I didn't mean –

SETH

– and the tighter you try to hold on, the faster it falls through your hands –

ESTHER

(*urgently*) – No, Dad, I was wrong, before. I ...

She scoops up a handful of earth and takes his hands so that they are holding it together.

Listen to me. I love this land, too: every field, every birch tree ... but, Dad ... I am a Dalzell. That's who I am. That's my inheritance. This ...

ESTHER squeezes SETH's hands as they hold the bit of soil.

... this ... is just dirt.

Pause. Together, they let the soil fall through their fingers to the ground.

SETH

Anthea. Tomorrow, we sell the farm.

Act II **Scene 8**

*Beginning of September 1982. Inside the kitchen of the
Dalzell home, barren but for boxes, are TODD and
ANTHEA. She is packing the Red Rose figurines in a small
box marked "Red Rose. Fragile."*

TODD

I still can't believe he's gone.

ANTHEA

I can't believe it's been a year already. Part of me keeps waiting for him to
come in from the field ...

> *Beat.*

At least it was quick. They said his heart just stopped, did I tell you that?
The night the sale went through ...

> *Pause.*

TODD

You're sure you don't need any help with your move?

ANTHEA

Oh, no, thank you. Everyone's coming straight from church tomorrow, we
could practically do a bucket brigade to my new apartment. They've all
been wonderful, I don't know how I would have gotten through it without
them. You know: "Pure religion and undefiled before God and the Father
is this ..."

TODD

"... to visit the fatherless and widows in their affliction, and to keep
himself unspotted from the world."

> *Beat.*

ANTHEA
> You'll have to come see the new place when I've got it all set up … and bring Esther.

TODD
> Certainly. I'd like that.

ANTHEA
> You'll make sure she goes to class every day?

TODD
> That won't be a problem. Weyburn Alternative is an exceptional school. She's going to love it there.

ANTHEA
> I hope so. I pray every day that I'm doing the … even though it …

TODD
> You're doing right by Esther.

ANTHEA
> My brothers and sisters in Christ don't think so. They don't understand it. I don't understand it. But …

> > *ESTHER comes down with a final suitcase. She may have pink hair or Joan Jett hair. Face paint and Doc Martens. She is definitely wearing black. Sweet sixteen.*

ESTHER
> Where's A.D.?

TODD
> He's packing your stuff in the trunk.

ESTHER
> Okay. Bye, Mom.

> > *Beat.*

ANTHEA
> You'll come back, you know.

> > *Beat.*

ESTHER
> Sure.

ANTHEA

Not at first. At first you'll feel really free. You'll see things I'll never see, you'll make more of yourself than I'll ever come to. Then you'll have your kids. You'll realize you don't know how to raise them in a box on the twenty-third floor. You'll want those kids to know the names of all the stars and all the trees and all their neighbours.

ESTHER

They have neighbours in the city, too, Mom. They have neighbourhoods. A neighbourhood is like a village.

Beat.

It's not like people here don't disappear.

ANTHEA

The difference is, here, when someone disappears, people notice.

ESTHER

I disappeared.

ANTHEA

I noticed.

A.D. appears in the doorway.

A.D.

Hey, Princess. We're good to go …

A.D. sees ANTHEA and walks over to her. She regards him uncertainly.

Been meaning to call you … no good at funerals … didn't know what to say … Mrs. Dalzell, I'm so sorry … uh … I'm sorry for your loss.

For the first time, she begins to let herself go, squeezing A.D.'s hands, then releasing them. TODD motions A.D. to go wait with him in the car. As they leave, ANTHEA collapses completely into ESTHER, who holds her.

ESTHER

THE LORD IS MY SHEPHERD …

Beat.

THE LORD IS MY SHEPHERD; I SHALL NOT WANT …

ESTHER AND ANTHEA

> HE MAKETH ME TO LIE DOWN IN GREEN PASTURES: HE
>   LEADETH ME BESIDE THE STILL WATERS.
> HE RESTORETH MY SOUL: HE LEADETH ME IN THE PATHS
>   OF RIGHTEOUSNESS FOR HIS NAME'S SAKE.
> YEA, THOUGH I WALK THROUGH THE VALLEY OF THE
>   SHADOW OF DEATH, I WILL FEAR NO EVIL: FOR THOU
>   ART WITH ME;
> THY ROD AND THY STAFF THEY COMFORT ME.
> THOU PREPAREST A TABLE BEFORE ME IN THE PRESENCE OF
>   MINE ENEMIES:

> *As ANTHEA continues the prayer, ESTHER silently
> detaches herself from her mother, shoulders her satchel, and
> starts toward the car.*

ANTHEA

> THOU ANOINTEST MY HEAD WITH OIL; MY CUP RUNNETH
>   OVER.
> SURELY GOODNESS AND MERCY SHALL FOLLOW ME ALL
>   THE DAYS OF MY LIFE:
> AND I WILL DWELL IN THE HOUSE OF THE LORD FOREVER.
> AMEN.

Act II **Scene 9**

*Much later. A crummy little room in a basement somewhere.
ESTHER leans forward on her crummy little chair.*

ESTHER

Hi. My name is Esther, this is my first time here, so ... I'm from a very
small town, and I never even knew there was such a thing as –

> *She consults a flyer.*

– "a youth study group for independent-minded Christians ..." So I read
the book for this week ... *Disappointment with God* ... and I – couldn't
stop crying ... Like the writer was whispering to me, "It's okay, you're not
alone ..."

> *Beat.*

I'm loving my life here. I love the music and the galleries ... I love the
energy of all these amazingly different people bumping around in a tiny
bit of space, trying to get along, trying all kinds of things ... but, and I
sure didn't see this coming ... I miss my church. I do. I miss that love. I
miss being part of the best club ever, where all I had to do was follow God
and spread the good news to everyone I met: we can all get to heaven,
and I've got the map.

> *Beat.*

I still believe in the map ... I THINK. I believe we're all trying to find our
way home. But it kind of doesn't make sense that the same directions will
work for everyone, does it? When we're all starting from a different place.

> *Beat. She opens her book.*

Okay: so, top of page seventy-four ... Is everyone with me? Great. I have
a question:

End of Act II

A Note about the Story

The first thing that drew me to the subject of a runaway teen was that I had written a story about adults in a rural community (*For Home and Country*) and about children (*Schoolhouse*), and it seemed time to look at someone who is negotiating the painful transition from childhood to adulthood. So I started speaking to young people in the rural communities around the 4th Line Theatre and the Blyth Festival … and I noticed an interesting phenomenon. At some point, I asked them all the same question: "If I asked you if you know anyone your age who is 'lost' … what would you say? Would that mean something to you?" Almost invariably, their faces and voices would get softer, their eyes would get wider and more faraway, and they would answer, singly or in groups, that, yes, they did know someone who was "lost" and, yes, they knew exactly what I meant.

A thoughtful study by Canada's Rural Partnership highlighted some of the concrete issues facing rural youth: "There has been for some time substantial concern regarding the loss of young people in rural communities. There is a sense that most rural communities offer few opportunities for their younger people, requiring them to leave for urban communities, most likely not to return." The study was called *Rural Youth: Stayers, Leavers, and Return Migrants*, and it identified some key factors in the decision all rural young people must make – to go, stay, or come back – a decision that an urban youth may not ever be conscious of making.

Like my previous plays for 4th Line and Blyth, *The Book of Esther* also explores different aspects of the urban–rural divide. Now, one of my favourite things about theatre is that you can get people in a room together who seem to be miles apart in every possible way and find reasons for them to stay there long enough to figure out what they have in common. (Or to kill each other … or, occasionally, both.) Theatre, of course, thrives on conflict. And since some of the most irreconcilable positions in my world seem to come from very conservative rural Christians and from militantly anti-religious urban queers, I thought I had an excellent place to start my play.

The trouble was, I didn't actually know very much about conservative (a.k.a. evangelical) Christians. I didn't even know any evangelical Christians, who are not exactly thick on the ground in the theatre world. And what I saw on Fox News and in the documentary *Jesus Camp* (2006) scared the stuffing out of me. So I spent a year doing a lot of reading – I can particularly recommend Lloyd Mackey's *These Evangelical Churches of Ours*, Mark A. Noll's *A History of Christianity in the United States and Canada*, and anything by Karen Armstrong or Philip Yancey.

At last, Eric Coates hooked me up with someone he barely knew himself: an elder in a local congregation, the intimidatingly named Huron Chapel Evangelical Missionary Church. Which is how I ended up in Elma Plant's kitchen, drinking a cup of coffee. "Why are you here?" she asked me, after I stirred in the cream and sugar.

She was much younger than I expected. About my age, in fact. She had a funky haircut. My hair looks like my mother cuts it, except my mother would do a much better job. "Sorry?"

"You're writing a play, you want to come to my church, you want to talk to my family ... I'm wondering why you are here."

"Oh. Well, the first thing I should say is that if I wanted to make fun of you or your religion, I wouldn't have taken two days to trek out to Blyth by public transit in the middle of February. I'd be mocking you from the comfort of my own home."

She waited while I took a sip of my coffee. It was excellent. "Okay. What's the second thing?"

"The second thing is that I am terrified of you."

"Me?! Why?"

"Because, as far as I can tell, the definition of an evangelical is that you are supposed to try and convert me. I'm terrified that, if I spend enough time with you and your church, I'm going to end up in Utah with a bump on my head, married to some guy who has seventeen wives, handing out tracts at airports. Also, I have many people in my life whom I love who are gay and lesbian, and I am worried that you are going to say something about them that is so offensive that I am going to have to walk out of here, and then I'll never write my play. I'm also terrified that I will write my play and you guys will burn down the theatre."

Elma stared at me, and spoke quietly and evenly. "My husband and I have been HIV-positive since 1981, and the gay community saved our lives. I vote NDP and I don't understand how anyone who calls himself a Christian could vote for anyone else. Don works with troubled teenagers, and we have been involved in AIDS education for more than twenty-five years. Does that help you at all?"

And it was at that moment – despite all the writerly angst and gnashing of teeth that would follow, despite my misgivings at how huge my subject was and how poorly equipped I was to handle it – that I knew I had to write this play.

Incidentally, I have still never been to Utah.

Acknowledgments

I began to work on *The Book of Esther* while I was the playwright-in-residence at the Blyth Festival, supported by the Canada Council for the Arts. My research and development continued while I was playwright-in-residence at the 4th Line Theatre, supported by the Ontario Arts Council. Then the play was work-shopped with the help of the Roulston Roy New Play Development Fund. Eric Coates and Deb Sholdice and all at Blyth – just like Rob Winslow, Kim Blackwell, Simone Georges, and all at 4th Line – have supplied me with stubborn faith and seventeen kinds of help. Thanks to the thoughtful artists who read the play in January 2010: Eric Coates, Marion Day, Alexis Hancey, Noah Reid, and Rick Roberts, directed by Leah Cherniak. Thanks also to the generous group who read the play for me in Niagara-on-the-Lake: Gord Bolan, Jeanie Calleja, Anthony Malarky, Tara Rosling, and Jonathan Tan. I cannot say enough about the team of actors who created those characters in that first production. They were smart, funny, passionate, and fearless; made wonderful suggestions about the text; and absorbed new cuts and even new scenes without complaint, as we all worked our hardest to ensure that every moment of this story was exactly what it needed to be. I was so proud of the look and sound of that production: the designers created two different worlds (city and country) that were by turns beautiful, haunting, and vibrant – and the crew toiled doggedly to realize all of our ambitious visions. Throughout the process it was my ridiculous good fortune to have Leah Cherniak putting all the pieces together – while always challenging me to go further, go deeper, go simpler. I was subsequently given the gift of a second production with Brad Rudy and his talented team bringing their own spin to the show, even with the added strain of having the author onstage. I am lucky to be published by the wonderful Talonbooks, where I have benefited from the eagle eye and thoughtful feedback of my editor, Ann-Marie Metten. I am, as always, indebted to my long-time dramaturg, Christine Sumption, for asking really hard questions and not giving me any of the answers.

This play would not have been finished without the legendarily inspirational Paula Vogel: three days with her at Playwrights Workshop Montreal were enough to get me past a writer's block the size of Saskatchewan, and I'll remember her kind encouragement forever.

I am so grateful to all the people I have interviewed over the past couple of years: Deb Sholdice and Sharon Thompson, whose reminiscences about their adolescence in Blyth in the 1980s reminded me so much of my own in Bewdley; Joan and Nick Whyte and their family (a Huron County poultry dynasty); veteran Cavan County family farmers Holly and Bob Hall as well as Cam and Eva Mary Bonner; Sergeant Arden Farrow of the Ontario Provincial Police, Huron

County Detachment, who filled me in on the legal and practical aspects of teenage runaways; Jeff McGavin of McGavin Farm Equipment in Walton, who helped me get the machinery right; farmer and banker Gord Wood of Kawartha Credit Union, who walked me through the 1980s Farm Crisis and the mechanics of financing and foreclosure; the Blyth Festival Young Company (especially Curtis te Brinke and Sarah Sholdice) and the students at Crestwood Secondary School in Peterborough and at Millbrook–South Cavan Public School, who spoke to me about their experiences as rural youth struggling to define their place in the world; and to everyone who came to the "community soundings" that the 4th Line Theatre held for me in Millbrook, Ontario, around the themes of life as a rural teenager and parenting a rural teenager. Thanks to everyone at the Huron Chapel Evangelical Missionary Church for welcoming me into their place of worship; to Jonathan Sy for his perspective on being part of a modern evangelical congregation; and to Gary Kirkham for insight on what it was like to leave one. Above all, thanks to the lovely, witty, and huge-hearted David Bateman, who began my political education; and to Elma Plant and her whole family for their stunning generosity in opening the doors of their home and their church to me – I truly cannot imagine how I could have written this story without them. As always, though, any errors are entirely my own.

A Cultural Timeline

February 8, 1980: Pierre Trudeau – only three months after "retiring" from politics – defeats Joe Clark to return as Canada's prime minister. The charismatic Trudeau is identified with massive government spending and is a social liberal who had declared in 1967 (while announcing his intention to decriminalize abortion, homosexuality, and divorce): "There's no place for the state in the bedrooms of the nation."

December 18, 1980: The prime lending rate hits 18.25%, as interest rates more than double 1976 levels in an attempt to beat inflation. For farm debt, which is considered higher risk, interest rates of 22% are not unusual. Coming on the heels of easy credit in the 1970s, when farmers were urged to borrow heavily from the banks in order to expand and modernize, this rise in interest rates precipitates a period of farm foreclosures and crippling debt known as the 1980s Farm Crisis. Suicides by North American farmers increase exponentially and, in many areas, small family farms are wiped out entirely, replaced by large commercial agribusinesses that can achieve economies of scale.

January 23, 1981: Joan Jett and the Blackhearts release the album *Bad Reputation* with a major label, after independently releasing it in 1980. The album cements Joan Jett's rep as the heir to Suzi Quatro and as one of the greatest rock 'n' roll guitar players of all time.

February 15, 1981: One hundred and sixty police officers arrest 286 men in a well-planned raid on four Toronto bathhouses in the Village, Toronto's gay district. One night later, thousands gather to protest in street demonstrations and mass meetings. Gays and Lesbians Against the Right Everywhere (GLARE) is formed. Future Toronto mayor Barbara Hall defends many of those arrested. It's a watershed moment in Canadian gay history that leads directly to Toronto's first Pride Day.

June 5, 1981: The U.S. Centers for Disease Control and Prevention publish a report about a troubling new disease that appears to be affecting American homosexuals.

June 28, 1981: At Grange Park, fifteen hundred people celebrate Toronto's first Pride Day.

July 29, 1981: HRH Charles, Prince of Wales, marries Lady Diana Spencer.

Further Reading

Armstrong, Karen. *The Battle for God*. New York: Anchor Books, 2001.

Bébout, Rick. Web memoir about Canada's gay mag *The Body Politic* and the culture it shaped. www.rbebout.com/.

Boyens, Ingeborg. *Another Season's Promise: Hope and Despair in Canada's Farm Country*. Toronto: Viking, 2001.

Campolo, Tony. Baptist minister and social justice activist, and friends. Blog. www.redletterchristians.org.

Canadian Advisory Council on the Status of Women. *Growing Strong: Women in Agriculture*. Ottawa: CACSW, 1987.

CBC News. Same-sex rights: Canada timeline. www.cbc.ca/news/background/ samesexrights/timeline_canada.html.

Dupuy, Richard, Francine Mayer, and René Morissette. *Rural Youth: Stayers, Leavers, and Return Migrants*. Analytical Studies Branch research paper series, no. 152. Ottawa: Statistics Canada, 2000.

Gilbert, Sky. *Ejaculations from the Charm Factory*. Toronto: ECW press, 2000.

Harris, Sam. *Letter to a Christian Nation*. New York: Vintage, 2008.

Mackey, Lloyd. *These Evangelical Churches of Ours*. Kelowna, BC: Wood Lake Books, 1995.

Noll, Mark A. *A History of Christianity in the United States and Canada*. Grand Rapids, MI: William B. Eerdmans Publishing, 1992.

Pope, Carole. *Anti Diva*. Toronto: Random House, 2000.

Xtra! Canada's Gay and Lesbian News. www.xtra.ca.

Yancey, Philip. *Disappointment with God: Three Questions No One Asks Aloud*. Grand Rapids, MI: Zondervan, 1988.
———. *Soul Survivor: How Thirteen Unlikely Mentors Helped My Faith Survive the Church*. Colorado Springs, CO: Waterbrook Press; (new edition) New York: Doubleday / London: Hodder Faith UK, 2003.
———. *What's So Amazing About Grace?* Grand Rapids, MI: Zondervan, 1997.

Leanna Brodie © Pierre Gautreau

LEANNA BRODIE is an actor, writer, and translator whose plays *For Home and Country, The Vic,* and *Schoolhouse* have been performed across Canada. (*Schoolhouse,* a critical and box office success in its runs at the 4th Line Theatre and at the Blyth Festival, has been produced almost constantly since 2006.) Her CBC radio dramas include *Invisible City* and *Seeds of Our Destruction.* She was the first Canadian invited to Seattle's ACT/Hedgebrook Women Playwrights Festival; has twice been Playwright-in-Residence at the Blyth Festival and 4th Line Theatre; and has belonged to the playwrights' units of the Tarragon Theatre and Theatre Passe Muraille – which co-produced her first play, *The Vic,* with Cahoots Theatre Projects.

She has translated plays, including Sébastien Harrisson's *From Alaska* (selected as the first project of the Quebec Translation Exchange between the Centre des auteurs dramatiques and the Banff Centre for the Arts); Hélène Ducharme's *Baobab* and *Tiger by the Tail*; Larry Tremblay's *Panda Panda*; Philippe Soldevila's *Tales of the Moon*; and Louise Bombardier's *My Mother Dog.*

Since attending Tapestry New Opera Works' renowned Composer-Librettist Laboratory, she has written libretti for Craig Galbraith, David Ogborn, and the New Zealand composer Anthony Young. Most recently, two works with Young have premiered in Auckland: *The Angle of Reflection* (Auckland Philharmonia Orchestra) and *Ulla's Odyssey* (The Opera Factory). Théâtre Motus continues to tour their acclaimed production of *Baobab* – a finalist for the Victor Prize at IPAY – throughout the United States and Canada.

Following on *For Home and Country* and *Schoolhouse, The Book of Esther* is the third play to centre on the fictional community of Baker's Creek. Developed through the 4th Line Theatre and Blyth Festival, all three share themes of acceptance versus exclusion, and explore different aspects of the rural–urban divide. Brodie's work is known for its strong focus on the voices of women.